Climbing Plants

ALREADY PUBLISHED

Growing Fuchsias
K. Jennings and V. Miller

Growing Hardy Perennials
Kenneth A. Beckett

Growing Dahlias
Philip Damp

Growing Irises
G. E. Cassidy and S. Linnegar

Growing Cyclamen
Gay Nightingale

Violets
Roy E. Coombs

Plant Hunting in Nepal
Roy Lancaster

The History of Gardens
Christopher Thacker

Slipper Orchids
Robin Graham with Ronald Roy

Growing Chrysanthemums
Harry Randall and Alan Wren

Waterlilies
Philip Swindells

The Rock Gardener's Handbook
Alan Titchmarsh

Better Gardening
Robin Lane Fox

IN PREPARATION

The Pelargonium Species
William J. Webb

Wine Growing in England
J.G. Barrett

1000 Decorative Plants
J. L. Krempin

Victorians and their Flowers
Nicolette Scourse

The Cottage Garden Year
Roy Genders

Growing Begonias
E. Catterall

Growing Bulbs
Martyn Rix

Country Enterprise
Jonathan and Heather Ffrench

Growing Roses
Michael Gibson

Climbing Plants

KENNETH A. BECKETT

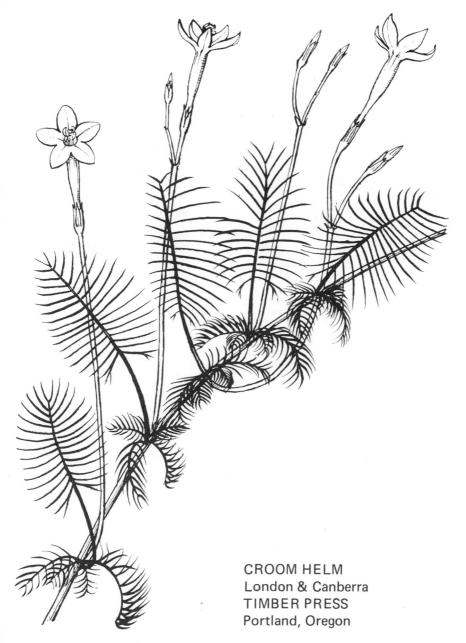

CROOM HELM
London & Canberra
TIMBER PRESS
Portland, Oregon

© 1983 Kenneth A. Beckett
Croom Helm Ltd, Provident House, Burrell Row,
Beckenham, Kent BR3 1AT

British Library Cataloguing in Publication Data

Beckett, Kenneth A.
　　Climbing plants.
　　1. Climbing plants
　　I. Title
　　582.1'8'01｜　　SB427

ISBN 0-7099-0687-0

First published in the USA in 1983 by Timber Press,
　PO Box 1631
Beaverton, OR97075
USA

ISBN 0-917304-76-4

Photographs by Gillian and Kenneth Beckett
Line Drawings by Geoffrey Herklots
Courtesy of Wm. Dawson & Sons, Publishers

For Moom

Printed and bound in Great Britain by
Biddles Ltd, Guildford and King's Lynn

Contents

Acknowledgements

For permission to use the line drawings which illustrate the text, I am much indebted to Dr Geoffrey Herklots. They were selected from the 270 drawings used to illustrate his own book *Tropical Flowering Climbers* published in 1976 by Dawson Science History Publications, to whom grateful thanks are due for allowing them to be used again here.

List of Figures

CHAPTER 1

Introduction

Honeysuckle, clematis and climbing roses around the door seem to be part of that romantically ideal garden so many of us strive to achieve. Climbing plants, if only in a limited way, do feature in most gardens and could be used more extensively and imaginatively. Of great appeal is their satisfying speed of growth. Many can well exceed 3 m in one growing season. For this reason they are splendid for beginners to gardening, especially children, but also for adults who have not yet gained that essential patience which dedication to gardening brings. More subjectively is the 'back to the jungle' appeal; primeval forest hung with rope-like lianes of tropical climbing plants. Fancifully atavistic perhaps, but the popularity of books and films with this aspect of wildlife as a theme or background is undeniable.

It is, of course, neither practical nor desirable to create an impenetrable jungle outside the back door. All we need is a reminder, and a short length of pergola, a latticed arbour or even a simple broad archway over a path or door will do for this nicely. Of these, the pergola has most to offer. Interwoven with a variety of species in all their colours, shapes and textures of leaf, flower and fruit, it provides one of the most satisfying of all plantings. One of its greatest appeals is the fourth dimensional one. A comparable planting of shrubs can only be viewed from the outside. A pergola enables us to see inside, a secluded jungly tunnel of co-existing plant life with great aesthetic appeal. Only here can the honeysuckle and rose, clematis and staff vine really get together and create a sort of living curtain that so much appeals to us in the wild.

Many people, some professional gardeners included, are dubious of or actually against putting climbers on house walls, particularly self-clingers such as ivy. Tales are told that the roots get into and damage foundations and that the clinging aerial roots break up the mortar between bricks. Climbers are also blamed as the harbingers of creepy-crawlies which then invade the house. I have been quite unable to find any real evidence to support these stories. The roots of most climbers are deeply delving and even if not, remain of relatively small diameter. The biggest temperate climbers are the wisterias and some specimens can develop almost tree-like main stems. Even so, root damage to foundations just does not occur.

The roots of ivy are very much surface stickers and are more likely to hold up a house rather than break it down. Many a picturesque ruined church tower owes its continued unchanging existence to a covering of ivy. The dense covering does indeed act as a cloak, protecting the masonry or brickwork from the errosively weathering effects of rain and snow, and insulating it against excessive heat and cold.

It is inevitable that a good growth of stems and foliage on a wall, particularly of the evergreen sort, will harbour wildlife, from spiders and insects to birds. As a result, a few extra spiders and other creatures may find their way into the house. Unless one is unnaturally biased against them, none should cause any alarm. Indeed, spiders as eaters of flies should be positively welcomed into the home.

Most of the books that have been written about climbing plants include also shrubs that can be trained out flat on or grown close to walls. This one does not. Only true climbers and their closely allied scramblers and trailers are dealt with. Previous books have been mainly concerned with hardy and half-hardy climbers with perhaps a few tender sorts that need glasshouse culture — at least in Britain. Here, I have included a good selection of tender climbers suitable for just frost-free to cool greenhouse conditions.

All the plants are given a hardiness zone rating so that readers of this book in countries other than Britain will know the temperature requirements of each plant described. Each number relates to a zone of the earth where the average absolute minimum temperature given in the zone table below can be expected in winter. This minimum temperature is calculated by averaging out the winter lows of 20 years. First worked out in the USA and more recently followed through to include Europe, this zonation concept can only be considered to give approximate hardiness ratings. Although low temperature is of great importance other factors also must be considered, such as the duration of a cold spell, whether conditions are windy or still, and whether cold was experienced gradually to allow acclimatisation, or suddenly. Ancillary to the wind factor is the degree of shelter afforded by larger plants, walls, fences and the general lie of the land. An additional, and surprisingly important factor, is the amount of summer sun and general warmth a plant receives prior to winter. Plenty of sunshine promotes well-ripened growth with good food reserves, notably a higher sugar content in the cell sap which then takes longer to freeze. If the summer has been poor, a partial remedy is to apply sulphate of potash at 10 g per square metre, in late summer. This will help to boost the amount of sugars and starches in the plant. Many half-hardy plants will stand having their tissues moderately frozen providing the thawing out is gradual. For this reason it is best not to site plants known to be a bit tender on east walls where the first rays of morning sun can get at them. This is especially relevant for plants with frost-tender young foliage and in areas that experience late spring frosts.

US Department of Agriculture Plant Hardiness Zones

	Fahrenheit	Centigrade
Zone 10	40° to 30°	4° to −1°
Zone 9	30° to 20°	−1° to −7°
Zone 8	20° to 10°	−7° to −12°
Zone 7	10° to 0°	−12° to −18°
Zone 6	0° to −10°	−18° to −23°
Zone 5	−10° to −20°	−23° to −29°
Zone 4	−20° to −30°	−29° to −34°
Zone 3	−30° to −40°	−34° to −40°

Note: Most of Britain falls into Zone 8.

Although the humid tropics is pre-eminently the home of climbing plants, the cooler temperate regions have plenty to offer the gardener. In the pages which follow, hundreds of different sorts are described. All are in cultivation and have been offered commercially somewhere or other during the past ten to fifteen years. Regrettably, at least 50 per cent of the plants listed are now difficult to obtain. The culture of young climbers is a labour-intensive occupation and the essential supporting, tying and pruning cannot be automated. Most nurserymen, therefore, tend to concentrate on the popular showy sorts like clematis and wisteria. Happily, some of the smaller, more dedicated nurserymen still maintain stocks of the less common climbers. If any reader seeking a particular rare or uncommon species has difficulty in obtaining it, I will gladly endeavour to find a source.

How they Climb

Climbers are the opportunists of the plant world, using their free-standing neighbours, mainly shrubs and trees, to reach the sun. Evolution, in its random manner, has seen to it that they achieve their ascent in a variety of intriguing ways. There are two primary requisites for a successful climber — speed of growth and a secure means for clinging to their hosts. The means involve four basic adaptations; twining stems, tendrils and adhesive aerial roots and hooks. Simplest and commonest is the twining stem, generally so efficient that one wonders why evolutionary quirks threw up the other three. Examples are many, from *Actinidia* (Chinese gooseberry) and convolvulus, to hop, runner bean and *Wisteria*. Depending on the genus and species, a twining climber encircles its host either clockwise or anti-clockwise. This is as much a fixed or inherited

11

Figure 1.1
Stem tip of *Manettia*
climbing in a
clockwise manner

⊢ INCH ⊣

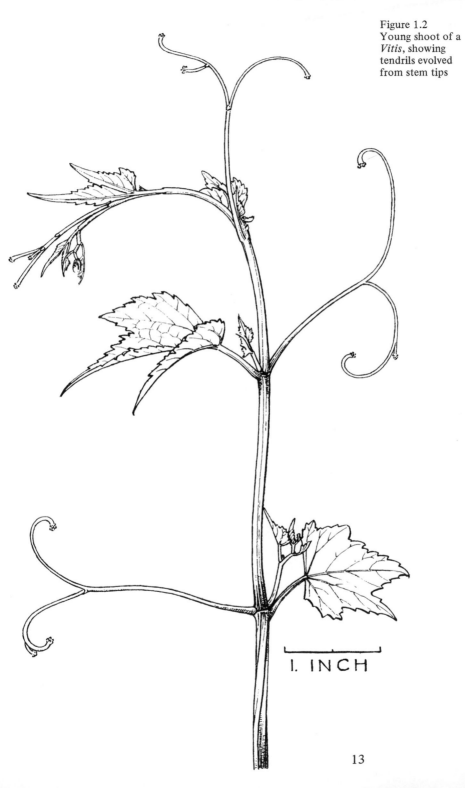

Figure 1.2
Young shoot of a
Vitis, showing
tendrils evolved
from stem tips

I. INCH

13

characteristic as leaf shape and flower colour. Convolvulus and runner bean for example, always twine to the left; hop and honey-suckle to the right. As in all things, however, there are exceptions. About 5 per cent of all climbing plant species don't seem to know which way to go, a stem first twining left then right. Such indecisive species are often poor climbers anyway, e.g. bittersweet or woody nightshade (*Solanum dulcamara*), described by Darwin as 'one of the feeblest and poorest of twiners' circling its host 'indifferently to the right or left'. The young and fast-growing tip of a twiner has surprising mobility, slowly moving round in a circle in search of a support. The shoot of a hop plant 35 cm long has been known to sweep round in a circle 47 cm in diameter in this quest. Once a support is found, the circle rapidly tightens, the cell tissue on the outside of the stem tip growing faster than that on the inside.

Next to the twiners come the tendril climbers. Tendrils are slender whip-like organs and are derived from both stems, stipules and leaves. The grape vine provides a good example of a stem tendril. Anatomically, this type of tendril is a stem tip, the stem itself elongating beyond it from an axillary bud in the leaf immediately below. The tendrils on marrow, cucumber and members of the same family (*Cucurbitaceae*) have the same origin.

Figure 1.3
Bignonia capreolata,
a single leaf showing
the upper leaflets
modified to tendrils

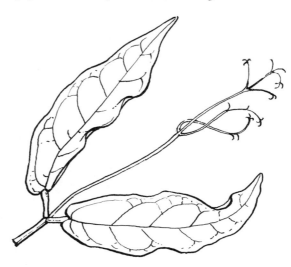

Sweet pea, garden pea, cup-in-saucer creeper (*Cobaea*) and Chilean glory flower (*Eccremocarpus*) provide familiar examples of tendrils derived from leaves. These are all plants with compound leaves and it is the terminal leaflets that become changed into tendrils. Once a tendril touches a support it circles around it firmly and soon thickens and becomes toughened with woody tissue. In some cases the tendril behind its point of attachment forms close spirals just like a bed-spring, pulling the plant nearer to its support. Many members of the cucumber family come into this category.

An interesting variation on a theme of leaf tendrils is provided by *Gloriosa* and *Sandersonia*. These have simple, narrow lily-like leaves which taper to a long, slender point with a hard recurved tip like a small cup-hook. Lashed in position by the wind, each hook may catch onto a support and then curl and tighten, but does not spiral. Another departure from the norm is the formation of small sucker discs on the tips of some tendrils. The best-known example is Virginia creeper (*Parthenocissus*), though the tendrils in this case are stem derived like the allied grape vine.

In some cases it is the leaf stalk which acts as a tendril. Garden nasturtium and other climbing sorts of *Tropaeolum* are the best examples. *Clematis* is almost in the same category, but here the leaf is compound and it is usually the stalks of the leaflets that do a half hitch around a likely support.

Many tropical climbers scale their jungle tree hosts by aerial roots, the house plants *Monstera* and the allied philodendrons being familiar examples. Much nearer home the ubiquitous ivy (*Hedera helix*) is a highly efficient root climber. So tightly do the small flattened roots adhere to their support that even if the stems are torn away the roots remain — even on such smooth, flat surfaces as paintwork.

In roses at least, the hooked prickles seem to be as much, if not more use as deterrents to browsing animals than as aids to climbing. Nevertheless the really vigorous, so-called climbing roses do scale and hold on to tree hosts by this means, often ascending 15-18 m or more. Hooks of this kind are derived from outgrowths of the skin or rind of a stem. Similar hooks also occur on leaf stalks or the backs of leaf mid-ribs and veins. The Costa Rican potato vine (*Solanum wendlandii*) and the over-familiar weed, goosegrass (*Galium aparine*) scramble and climb most efficiently by this means. Other examples, mostly from warm countries, bear hooks derived from leaflets or stipules (small leaflet-like organs at the base of a leaf stalk). Wonderfully equipped in this way are the climbing tropical palms known as rattans, the leaf tips of which resemble whips set with many pairs of twin fish hooks (modified leaflet pairs). These lash about in the wind and soon become securely entangled among surrounding tree branches. Less flamboyantly efficient is the cat's-claw vine (*Doxanthera unguis-cati*). Here, the three terminal leaflets of each leaf are transformed into small, slender hooks with points so fine and hard that they can cling firmly to brick and stone surfaces.

Scramblers

There is a further category of climbers which at first glance, and particularly to the novice, appears to have no special adaptations. These are the scramblers. To behave as climbers they need the overhead support of a well-branched shrub or tree. Once established they throw up robust, but pliable, stems which push up through the branches above like a needle through a tangle of knitting wool. This holds them temporarily, then side branches grow out at right angles, or even inclined downwards to prevent slipping back or sideways. Most of the best examples are found in the warmer countries, the most generally familiar being *Allamanda cathartica* and the Canary Island bellflower, *Canarina canariensis.*

CHAPTER 2

Climbers at Home

In the wild, the majority of climbers are restricted to forests and areas of scrub. Presumably they evolved the climbing mode of life amid such taller plants to reach the light, and they remain inseparable. Some of the smaller climbers are found among herbaceous plants, but they are very much in the minority. Like all other plant categories, the climbers fit neatly into their habitat, but whether annuals, herbaceous perennials or shrubs they need the support of nearby, free-standing plants. To see how climbers fit into their native terrain we need familiar surroundings to look at. The continent of Europe, of which Britain is very much a part in many ways, particularly floristically, provides examples of all the main sorts of climbers and scramblers. A start can be made by studying a weedy waste plot or overgrown garden. Here, almost certainly, will be seen examples of annual and perennial climbers and the way they exploit their self-supporting neighbours. Widespread, though rarely abundant is black bindweed (*Polygonum convolvulus*). It is technically a climbing annual knotgrass, but with its heart-shaped leaves and twining stems well merits the species name *convolvulus*, and vernacular bindweed. Depending on soil and situation its stems grow 30-120 cm long and rapidly lace together the nearby weeds — and garden plants. The small, whitish flowers are insignificant, but attractive to bees. It is, in effect, a diminutive annual version of the rampageous Russian vine (*Polygonum (Bilderdyckia) baldschuanicum*). Equally common on waste ground, in gardens and hedgerows is the ubiquitous goosegrass or cleavers (*Galium aparine*), sometimes named also as sweethearts and such lovely old names as hayriff, cling rascal, gentlemen's tormentors and many others. Despite the tininess of the hooks on its leaves and stems, it is a most efficient climber, weaving webs of growth difficult to remove as anyone will know who has tried to pull it out of a garden hedge or choice flowering shrub.

Among perennial climbers that can associate with the annuals, the best known is lesser bindweed (*Convolvulus arvensis*). With its wide open, pink to white funnel-shaped flowers this is an attractive plant especially when making flat mats of leafage as it will when there is no support available. In the garden it is an almost ineradicable weed and its tightly twining wiry stems make a mess of choice herbaceous plants. Also a weed but just as common in the hedgerow is its lovelier, but just as deadly, large-flowered cousin, hedge bindweed (*Calystegia sepium*) and the even bigger-bloomed large bindweed (*C. sylvatica*). These can reach 3 m or more in height and do a thorough job of tying together stems of perennials, shrubs and small trees.

Hedgerows are essentially man-made features but they harbour many wild plants and animals, most of them originally woodland dwellers. Several climbers are now almost restricted to, or are largely found in, hedges or nearby areas of scrub. Black and white bryony are two good examples of herbaceous perennials. Despite the similar vernacular names they are widely different to look at and poles apart from a botanical point of view. Black bryony (*Tamus communis*) is a stem twiner and a member of the tropical yam family (*Dioscoreaceae*). It has smooth, glossy, heart-shaped leaves, tiny greenish flowers and quite large, glossy red berries. White bryony (*Bryonia dioica*) is a member of the largely tropical cucumber family (*Cucurbitaceae*). Climbing by stem tendrils it has hand-shaped, somewhat hairy leaves, whitish-green flowers and pea-sized red fruits. Both seldom grow more than 3-5 m in a season, dying back to tuberous roots set deeply in the hedge bottom or among the roots of a shrub or tree. Often associating with the bryonies are dog rose and honeysuckle, two of the most familiar woody-stemmed climbers. Honeysuckle (*Lonicera periclymenum*) spirals tightly around its host stems and often puts on a real stranglehold, biting deeply into its support. Hazel and other stems deformed into a spiral pattern by honeysuckle are the basis of corkscrew walking sticks. Honeysuckle can be a great lacer up of trees and shrubs and in some woodlands is a pest. Wild or dog rose (*Rosa canina*) is barely a climber when confined by the hedge slashers. Among tall scrub or in woodland edges and rides it will send up erect young shoots 4-6 m. There, held by its hooks, it branches and arches downwards most effectively though by no means so spectacularly as such real climbing roses as *R. filipes* 'Kiftsgate'.

Wet or damp woodland, especially the continuously saturated sort designated as carr is the home of several climbers. In Britain and much of Europe it is the only habitat that gives some idea of a tropical jungle in miniature. It is often dense and humid with the stems clothed in mosses and lichens. Adding to the tangle are such climbers as the common hop *Humulus lupulus*, the weakly climbing bittersweet or woody nightshade (*Solanum dulcamara*), hedge bindweed and others. Despite this, the only European climber to create a jungle-like liane grows in drier woods, usually on limy soils.

This is old man's beard (*Clematis vitalba*), better known in Britain as a hedgerow plant. Given the opportunity, however, and the time it can grow by way of its tendril-like leaflet stalks to 30 m in length with looping stems as thick as a man's arm. Also found in hedges but very much a denizen of the forest is common ivy (*Hedera helix*). This splendid and highly variable evergreen root climber will soar high up into the crown of a tree, certainly to about 30 m. Although in time its stems will completely clothe trunk and branches, ivy seldom links several trees together and never forms a liane. Contrary to popular belief it is seldom responsible for a tree's demise, though the added weight may help bring down an ancient or ailing tree in a storm.

This brief survey hopefully gives some idea of the better known climbing plants of western Europe and particularly Britain, and how they grow in the wild. Eastern Europe, Asia and North America can offer more numerous and often bigger examples in a greater variety of genera and families. The same is also true of the equivalent latitudes in the Southern Hemisphere, though here, many of the genera and families are quite different from those north of the equator. However varied botanically they may be, the same modes of climbing will be found and the same impetuous hurry to grow up and reach the sun.

CHAPTER 3

Uses in the Garden

Among the various categories of garden plants, few are more adaptable and generally useful than the climbers. Not only do they perform in their accepted role, but some at least provide excellent ground cover when allowed to grow flat on the ground. An ivy-carpeted woodland area bears testimony to this. Others, notably wisteria and *Hydrangea petiolaris* can, with some pinching and pruning, be grown free-standing, then ranking with some of the best of shrubs.

Purely as climbers, there is a variety of situations around the garden that they can fill with distinction as no other group of plants can. For me they have three primary roles; clothing house walls, forming the living fabric of a pergola and lending beauty or contrast to an otherwise dull tree. A house very much needs to be merged or incorporated into the planting scheme of the garden. Basically this is done with a planting of shrubs at the foot of the walls. In the USA this has come to be called a foundation planting, an apt and descriptive term we might well adopt more widely in Britain. The complete marrying of house and garden only really comes about when climbers are planted with the shrubs and trained up high onto the walls behind. For a house of no special architectural beauty or historical interest the aim can be a mosaic of plants to cover all but the windows. Providing the walls are sound to start with, climbers can do no harm. Indeed, a good clothing of plants will protect the wall from weathering and give an extra layer of insulation. In general, it is best to confine climbers to the wall. Once onto the roof they can get under tiles and block gutterings. Where the architecture is worth exhibiting, one or two choice, smaller growing plants can be used to enhance it. At least a proportion of evergreens should be used to maintain the effect in winter.

Garden walls, fences and screens offer the same sort of planting opportunities, but the general lack of height tends to limit the choice of species. Nevertheless, there are plenty of smaller growing subjects which will quickly transform a bare, plain or ugly wall or fence into a feature of beauty.

For those to whom climbers have a strong appeal, the erection of some sort of pergola is a must. It need not be elaborate; at its simplest no more than a few arches over the path from gate to house. Arbours, gazebos and garden sheds are all the better for a clothing of climbers. If none of these structures are present, then tripods or single rustic poles can be sited strategically as supports for the smaller species. Tripods can be very effective to lend height to a shrub or mixed bed or border.

The most natural way of staging a climber is to grow it up a living tree. Well done, it creates a wonderfully dramatic effect and really brings a breath of the wild wood into the garden. Unlike the pergola, this method highlights one tree and one or two climbers, the ensemble becoming a specimen planting or focal point. For this reason the climbing partner must be chosen with care to combine or contrast with its host. Obviously it is not recommended to use a rare or choice tree that is highly decorative in its own right. The most likely candidate will be an unproductive fruit tree, probably an apple. Trees with a heavy leaf canopy such as sycamore, maple and plane should be avoided, as the climber will not get enough light for satisfactory growth.

Using a dead tree, either with the main branches left or shortened back, is not so effective as a living one, but it does provide a good framework for supporting a wide variety of less high flying climbers, particularly roses, ivies, honeysuckles, *Pileostegia viburnoides*, *Solanum crispum* and others.

Hedges and specimen shrubs are all too often neglected as supports. Providing the hedge type and climber are matched carefully, some really striking effects can be produced. Well tried is the Chilean flame creeper (*Tropaeolum speciosum*) flaring its way up a dark green yew or holly hedge. Other *Tropaeolum* species such as the annual yellow *T. peregrinum* would make another eye-catching association, or one could use the even showier yellow *Thladiantha* or the orange-red *Eccremocarpus*. Some of the smaller growing clematis, especially the *C. viticella* hybrids, also look splendid scrambling over a hedge.

Every greenhouse, however small, deserves at least one ornamental climber, that is of course unless food plants such as tomatoes are the over-riding priority. Occupying the normally empty roof space, a climber, preferably planted in a ground level bed, can give a greenhouse that furnished look the year round. If one with a light foliage cover is chosen, say *Jasminum polyanthum* or *Plumbago capensis*, then a natural shading is provided for other plants beneath, doing away with blinds or painting the glass with 'Summer cloud' or a similar preparation. I prefer climbers which look good in winter and early spring when there is not much doing outside. Nothing can be nicer than to enter the protected environment of a greenhouse on a late winter's day to be greeted by the perfume of the jasmine mentioned above.

CHAPTER 4
Cultivation

As we have seen, climbers in the wild are always closely associated with the plants they rely upon for support. The majority originate in forests and scrub, their roots delving into the humus-rich, usually moist and relatively cool soil. These are the sort of conditions then that we must aim for in the garden. Happily, there are very few soils that cannot be made suitable for climbers. Indeed, with the regular application of water to very porous soils in low rainfall areas, there are none. Water is the one element in the successful cultivation of climbers which must never be in short supply. Their high speed of growth makes it imperative that there is always a regular flow of water to the growing points. Given sufficient water, most climbers will grow reasonably well even in quite poorish soils. For really healthy growth and a good floral display, however, a fertile soil is necessary. Thin sandy soils and the harsher types of clay can easily be made acceptable by the liberal application of organic matter. This comes in a variety of guises from rich farmyard manure to moss peat and such waste products as spent hops. Rotted farmyard manure is by far the best, with garden compost and leafmould good runners-up. Peat is also good but has very little food value and needs to be accompanied with fertiliser. Broken down by minute bacteria and fungi, organic matter provides humus, a colloidal substance and the key to soil fertility.

As climbers are rarely grown *en masse*, it is not necessary to provide large areas for planting as one might, say, for a shrub border. Site preparation for each plant is enough. Where a climber is to be set at the foot of a wall, this sort of soil preparation is most important. The soil at the base of house walls, particularly of new properties, is often compounded of subsoil and rubble. As much of the latter as possible must be removed and replaced with better soil from another part of the garden or elsewhere. If only subsoil remains, some can be removed and the remainder liberally mixed with organic matter; two to three 2 gal bucketsful per square metre will not be too much. Where a large-growing climber such as *Wisteria* or *Celastrus* is being grown, it is worthwhile improving a full square metre at

23

30 cm deep for each plant; 60 cm square is adequate for the smaller species. If the soil is in a reasonable state then 45 cm square, and one bucketful of organic matter is enough. Where the soil is known to be in a good fertile state, no special preparation is necessary, though it is always worthwhile adding extra humus to the planting hole. If specimen climbers are to be set in a lawn, a circular bed at least 60 cm across and 30 cm deep must be made. The grass is skimmed off, chopped up and placed in the bottom of the hole and the soil is returned mixed with organic matter.

Drainage

Although climbing plants need plenty of water during the growing season, very few appreciate permanently wet, i.e. waterlogged conditions. Poor drainage is rarely a serious problem in most gardens, but where it is, a means must be found to provide a less wet site. The easiest way is to create a raised bed 30-45 cm deep and at least 60 cm or more square. This can be retained by bulks of timber, stone, brick, peat blocks etc. The more labour intensive method is to lay tile drains. This will also involve digging a sump hole if there is no natural lower outlet for surplus water. It is not necessary to drain a large area, and drainage pipes can be laid to run from the bottom of each planting hole to a centrally sited sump or outlet. The latter will need to be excavated several feet lower than the planting holes.

Planting
Distances

Climbers are invariably sold in containers and can be put into their permanent sites at any time, providing soil conditions are right. Wet and frosty conditions should be avoided and in areas of dry springs, early autumn planting is recommended. There is no set distance apart at which to plant climbers. Much depends on what sort of ultimate effect is required; whether each one is to be treated as a single specimen or several are to be grown harmoniously inter-mingling. As specimens, a suitable distance apart should be not less than half the ultimate height of the species chosen.

Supporting

All climbing plants need support for life, so whatever means is chosen must be secure. Wooden stakes, posts and trellis work should be treated thoroughly with a preservative. Poles should be sturdy and set deeply, ideally in a concrete base. Pergolas in particular, when covered with verdure, not only have to support a considerable weight but act as wind barriers. The same is true of single poles or tripods, though in a lesser way. Where walls and fences are the primary support, strong galvanised wire and eyed bolts (vine eyes) should be used, the latter embedded in rawlplugs. Tall tree stumps can be prepared in the same way, the wires soon being covered with stems and leaves. It may be necessary to use one or two eyed bolts in the trunk of a living tree if this method of growing is adopted, but ideally, this should be avoided. A strong cane, rope or chain secured to the first branch is the best way of starting a climber on its way.

The planting procedure is straightforward. A hole is dug a little deeper and wider than the root ball. If the soil has not been previously prepared, some peat or decayed manure and a general fertiliser should be forked into the bottom of the hole and mixed with some of the removed soil. The plant is set in position just a little deeper than the top of the root ball and filled around with soil. Small plants can be firmed with fists, larger ones with the foot. In dry areas the planting should be finished to leave a very shallow saucer-shaped depression around the plant to facilitate watering. If the climber is to be set at the base of a wall or high fence make sure it will not be in a rain shadow either from the sheer height of the structure or from overhanging eaves. It is wise to plant not closer than 30 cm from the support unless one is prepared to water regularly during dry spells for the first one to two years or until roots have spread well out into the garden.

Planting Procedure

Extra thought must be given to the planting of a climber destined to ramble through a living tree. Although the root systems of climbers are adapted to co-exist with those of shrubs and trees, better initial growth will be made if the competition factor can be reduced. There are two positions where a climber can be planted, right at the base of the trunk where the tree's feeding roots are minimal or non-existent, or several feet beyond the tree's canopy of branches where the feeding roots thin out. Some trees make a close mesh of feeding roots near the soil surface; for example, common ash (*Fraxinus excelsior*) and sycamore (*Acer pseudoplatanus*), and planting the climber beyond the branch canopy is best. Many other trees, e.g. apple, cherry, oak, have more deeply delving roots and the climber is best at the trunk base. If there is any doubt about the vigour of the tree roots, the sides of the planting hole can be lined with plastic sheeting and the hole filled with heavily humus-enriched soil.

After planting, it is not enough for the climber's continuing welfare to let it fend for itself. Watering is important during all dry spells during the first year. This is especially important if the plant was pot bound or very well rooted at planting time. Feeding also must

After-care

25

not be neglected. For the first few years at least a general fertiliser in spring is very beneficial. The modern slow-release granular sorts are particularly recommended. In the wild, climbers receive an annual mulch of fallen leaves from the surrounding shrubs and trees. In the garden, a mulch of organic matter each spring will ensure that the soil is kept cool, moist, and well supplied with humus. If pulverised bark direct from Forestry Commission depots is used as a mulch it is essential to dress it immediately with a nitrogenous fertiliser. The bacteria of decay which break down all organic matter need nitrogen to work. The more raw the state of the organic matter, e.g. bark, the more nitrogen is needed and the soil quickly drained of this essential plant food. Without adequate nitrogen, no climber can grow the way it should.

Winter
Protection

With a little ingenuity, it is possible to provide protection which will ensure the survival of half-hardy plants outside in Britain in all but the coldest winters. The essential factor is protection from freezing winds and these generally come from a northerly direction, from NE round to NW. Heavy duty polythene is useful for this sort of protection, though ventilation must be given on all mild days or the sheeting perforated, to prevent excessive condensation. Bracken and straw are effective insulators and if sandwiched between two layers of chicken wire (wire netting) laced together with galvanised wire or binder twine, can be made into mats and collars. Mats can be hung in front of climbers on walls, and crescent-shaped collars placed around the stem base and pushed up tight to the wall or fence. Roots are often more tender than the tops and it is important to insulate the soil surface over the root area. Dry bracken, dead oak or beech leaves can be put down as a mulch and held in place with chicken wire. Alternatively, grit, gravel, coarse sand, weathered ashes, peat or pulverised tree bark can be used. By such means, half-hardy plants can be brought through the average hard winter provided the periods of day and night continuous freezing do not persist at disastrously low levels for more than a week or so.

Cultivation
under Glass

Basically, the cultivation of climbing plants under glass is the same as for the open garden. There are, of course, the added factors of growing them in containers and of maintaining a suitable temperature. In addition, there is much less space for the plants to expand so pruning may have to be more restrictive.

Although much depends on the size of the greenhouse and vigour of the climber chosen, in general it is more satisfactory to grow the plant in a floor level bed. For this method, the comments on soil

26

improvement for the open garden equally apply. In the smaller greenhouses, certainly those less than 2.4 x 2 m it is wise to confine a climbing plant to a container. The lightweight plastic pots and tubs are ideal, and those in the range 30-35 cm the most useful. Almost any of the proprietary potting composts are suitable, but a loam-based, e.g. John Innes potting No. 2 or 3, usually gives the best results. Garden soil can be used but it must be enriched with organic matter and fertilisers. Because the root system of a plant in a pot is closely confined to a much less volume of soil than it would occupy in the garden, a rich growing medium is necessary. As a rough guide, garden soil should be mixed with equal parts of organic matter. To this mixture must be added a good general fertiliser, preferably of the slow-release sort. Support systems as used in the garden can also be used under glass. The neatest and most efficient method is eyed bolts and galvanised wire along the sides and roof of the greenhouse. Very small climbers, e.g. *Tropaeolum tricolorum*, can be trained over a balloon of wires or twiggy sticks stuck in the compost near the pot rim.

Spring is the best time for setting young plants in their beds or flowering-sized containers, but this can be done at almost any time of the year. Plants in beds outside should be fed and mulched. Plants in containers will need top-dressing in autumn or spring. This involves the stripping away of surplus compost and roots to a depth of at least 5 cm and re-placing with fresh compost. Plants established in their containers for more than two years will benefit from liquid feeding at monthly intervals from late spring to autumn.

Watering must be attended to regularly. In summer this will mean a daily or twice daily measure of water, at least during hot spells. In winter, once a week or less may be sufficient. If there is any doubt as to whether a plant needs water, scratch down about 1 cm into the compost with a finger tip. If the compost feels dry at this depth, the plant needs watering.

Pruning

Whether outside or under glass, most climbers will need pruning, if only to curtail their exuberant growth from time to time. Where the height of the support is limited, especially if less than the growth potential of the climber, some early pruning is advantageous. This will encourage branching low down and prevent the formation of long, bare stems. A start should be made at planting time or the spring following, by reducing the height of the young plant by half. Subsequent young stems should have their growing points pinched out at 30 cm. Further pinching may be necessary to stimulate adequate branching low down. Trained, and if necessary tied into position, these initial branches will become the framework of the

27

mature climber. Once this framework is established, pruning is best confined to after flowering or during the dormant or resting winter period. After flowering, pruning consits of removing spent flower clusters with a short length of stem. In addition, some congested stems can be thinned out. Winter pruning consists largely of thinning. Where there are plenty of stems at or near ground level, it is best to remove whole branches rather than lots of young stems higher up. Very vigorous climbers in confined quarters will need drastic pruning. All the previous season's stems are best cut back by at least two thirds, leaving only the basic framework and their laterals. Many climbers are not easy to deal with in this way, the wiry-stemmed twiners and self clingers for example. On the other hand they can be left to grow unpruned, often for many years. On walls, such climbers are best kept pruned or sheared away from gutterings, tiled roofs and window embrasures. It is hardly possible and seldom desirable to prune climbers growing through trees. The more specialised pruning methods that some climbers require, e.g. clematis, are described in the relevant generic entry.

Propagation

Increasing one's favourite plants, either to replace an old specimen that has outgrown its allotted space, or to give to friends, is a very satisfying aspect of gardening in general. Many climbers are easily propagated with a minimum of equipment, though some sort of propagating case for cuttings is worthwhile. This can be improvised from a seed tray or shallow box covered with plastic sheeting supported on U-shaped lengths of galvanised wire. Single pots can be placed in polythene bags. Even better are the rigid, clear plastic covers of various sizes usually sold with a basal tray. Such a unit with an electric heating cable in the bottom will be necessary for the more difficult cuttings, and certain seeds. The primary methods of increasing climbers are as follows:

Division

Those climbers which make several to many stems from ground level or below can often be divided into two or more rooted pieces, e.g. *Aconitum*, *Asparagus*, *Codonopsis*, *Convolvulus*, *Lathyrus*. The plants are lifted in late winter or early spring and either carefully pulled or cut apart, the divisions being immediately replanted.

Layering

Climbers more readily lend themselves to this method of propagation than most other plant groups. Layering is the practice of inducing a stem to produce roots while still attached to the plant. This means getting the chosen stem down to ground level, and the more flexible it is the easier the task. Healthy one-year-old stems are chosen, preferably in spring, and brought down to ground level at the easiest point. The soil at this point is forked over and, if of a sticky nature, mixed with coarse sand. A depression 5-7.5 cm deep is then made to take the layer. The stem is bent into a U-shape so that the base of the U rests on the base of the depression. A small notch, nick or slice is made at the bottom of the U and dusted with a hormone rooting powder. Although not always necessary, it is best to anchor the layer with a forked stick or bent wire pushed in at the base of the U. Soil is filled in over it level with the surrounding soil and the free tip of the layer tied to a cane. About 9-12 months need to elapse before the layer is rooted and can be severed from the parent plant and transplanted.

Cuttings

Many climbers can be increased very easily from stem cuttings and a few from root cuttings. In each case these are severed pieces of young stem or root which are induced to grow on their own. Stem cuttings are of two basic types, dormant and generally leafless (except some evergreens), and growing and leafy. Dormant cuttings are made from mature one-season stems in autumn or early winter. These are usually described as hardwood cuttings. Sections of stem 20-30 cm long are made, severed cleanly beneath a node and inserted in sandy soil for two thirds of their length. They can be inserted directly into the growing site or in a nursery plot to grow on for a year. Species of *Vitis* can be taken as single bud cuttings or eyes. These are made from mature stems in winter or early spring, the prominent buds being cut out with about 2 cm of stem on either side. A thin slice of each section is removed from the side opposite the bud and this cut surface is gently pressed down horizontally into a small, loosely filled pot of rooting compost and placed in a heated propagating case.

Leafy cuttings are of two types, softwood and semi-hardwood. Softwood cuttings are taken in early summer or while the current season's shoots are still soft and sappy. Semi-hardwood cuttings are taken in late summer or early autumn, selecting shoots that are woody at the base but softer above. Both sorts of cuttings can be trimmed in one of two ways, beneath a node or leaf, and with a heel. The latter can be gently pulled from the parent stem, but if it is at all possible it is best to cut them off with a slicing motion, using a razor blade or sharp knife. Nodal cuttings are satisfactory for most climbers, but a few of the more difficult to root species respond

29

best if made with a heel. About 10 cm (4 in) is an average length for a leafy cutting but stems of climbers often have very long internodes and up to 15 cm (6 in) may be necessary. A cutting should have a node at the top and bottom, and ideally at least, one more node in the middle. Some species, e.g. clematis, can be propagated with one node at the top, the base of the cutting being cut between nodes — an internodal cutting. About half of the stem of each cutting should be inserted into the rooting medium. Clematis also root very successfully as single bud cuttings similar to those described above for *Vitis*, but taken in summer with a leaf or part of a leaf retained (leaf budcuttings). The use of a hormone powder is recommended. All leafy cuttings require a propagating case and a sharply draining compost. The latter is easily made by mixing equal parts of moss peat with coarse sand, grit or perlite.

Seeds

What a satisfying boast it is to point to a big climber either touching the eaves of the house or cascading from a tree 12 m up and say, 'I grew that from seed'. Sowing seeds and rearing the subsequent seedlings to maturity can be a most rewarding pastime and needs no more equipment than pots and pans and compost.

There are several special soil mixtures commercially available for seed sowing. If one has a lot of seeds to sow they are probably worth obtaining, though potting compost is just as effective. The advantages of these proprietary mixes is that they are partially sterilised and do not contain weed seeds or pest and disease organisms. Small pots or pans 7.5-13 cm wide are the ideal containers. Crocking or drainage material is not necessary. Each pot is filled and lightly firmed so that there is a 2 cm gap between the soil surface and the rim of the container. The seeds must be sown thinly. If they are large enough to handle with the fingers or tweezers and time and patience allow, there is much to be said for sowing individually (space-sowing). Very fine seeds can be mixed with several volumes of fine sand and the mixture scattered thinly. Never cover seeds deeply. Over-deep sowing is responsible for more disappointment than any other cause. As a rough guide, most seeds should be covered with compost to a depth equalling that of their widest diameter. Very fine seeds do not need covering. After sowing, either water with a fine-rosed can or immerse them in a tray of water to just below the pot rim until thoroughly moist, then remove and drain. If the seeds are sown in spring they are best put in a frame or greenhouse or on a shady window ledge indoors. Freshly gathered seeds, particularly those in berries, are best plunged outside in a sheltered, shaded spot and the compost surface topped with fine gravel to prevent panning in torrential rain. Berried seeds should be extracted from the pulp and space-sown. If large quantities are to be dealt with then they can be bruised and mixed with several parts of moist soil (stratifying). The whole lot can then be sown thinly, or first put through a sieve, then sown in late winter or early spring. Like those of hardy trees and shrubs, the seeds of some climbers have built in dormancy factors that ensure their germination at the most propitious time. In some cases the seed coats contain chemical germination inhibitors which leach out during the winter rains. Others need a cool to cold period after sowing to break dormancy. Seeds with these sorts of requirements are usually easy to germinate if sown fresh from the plant. If allowed to dry out for several weeks or months, they can take a year or more to germinate.

As soon as seedlings are seen crooking through the soil they must be brought into good light so that they will develop sturdily. When the seedlings are large enough to handle, and before they get crowded, they must be pricked off into individual small pots; 7.5 cm diameter is the most useful size. An approved potting mix must be used; the John Innes potting No. 2 is good. Some climbers start to elongate rapidly in the seedling stage; others, e.g. *Eccremocarpus*, build up a rosette or tuft of leaves first, then grow fast. Either way, slender canes or twiggy sticks will be needed for support. The really quick growers can be planted into their flowering sites as soon as the pots are full of roots. Slower growing kinds are best potted-on into larger containers, e.g. 13-15 cm diameter, and plunged outside in a sheltered place until the following spring.

Pests and Diseases

Surprisingly few of the known pests and diseases of hardy plants attack climbers. Aphids, capsid bugs and earwigs are the commonest pests, mildew and rose black spot the most prevalent fungus diseases. The following list is based on observed symptoms and suggested controls. When chemical insecticides and fungicides are necessary, always follow the maker's instructions to the letter. An overdose could harm the plant, an underdose will probably leave the pest largely unharmed.

Leaves deformed

Curled, twisted and crumpled leaves, especially at the shoot tips, usually denotes an attack of aphids (blackfly and greenfly). These are tiny, oval, soft bodied creatures usually in crowded clusters. There are winged and wingless forms and they vary in body colour from green to yellowish, pinkish, greyish and black. They suck plant sap, severely crippling and weakening the stems. Many proprietary

31

insecticides are available to deal with them, notably malathion, derris, pyrethrum and pirimicarb. See also *Leaves with spit-like frothy masses*.

If young leaves look somewhat tattered or have irregular holes, capsid bugs are the likely culprits. These are rather like large, flattened, fast moving aphids, but secretive and not commonly recognised. HCH (BHC), dimethoate and fenitrothion are the best insecticides.

Leaves eaten

Pieces eaten out of leaves generally signifies the feeding of a caterpillar or earwig. Irregular or ragged appearance is more likely to be an earwig. Clematis and other species on rustic poles and pergolas are very prone, the nocturnal earwigs resting under the bark during the day. HCH (BHC), malathion, carbaryl and pirimiphos-methyl are the main cures for earwigs. These and many other substances will also kill caterpillars.

Leaves mottled

A fine light mottling progressively followed by bronzing and withering or leaf fall denotes the presence of glasshouse red spider mite. Although mainly a greenhouse pest, it can overwinter in warm, sheltered places and is sometimes a nuisance on wall climbers. The creature is a minute spider ally, up to 0.5 mm long, yellowish or greenish, with or without red markings, the females bright red in autumn. Control is not easy but the active mites are killed by malathion, formothion, diazinon and dicofol.

Leaves rolled

The leaflets of all sorts of roses may become tightly rolled soon after they reach full size in May and June. This is the work of the leaf-rolling rose sawfly and while it does little harm it creates an unsightly effect. Picking off the rolled leaves is the most efficient method of control. Alternatively, apply one of the systemic insecticides such as dimethoate or formothion.

Leaves with scales

See *Stems with scales*.

Leaves with sooty film

An often puzzling sooty coating sometimes appears on leaves with no obvious cause. It invariably occurs on climbers in or beneath lime trees (*Tilia*) or sycamore maple (*Acer pseudoplatanus*) which are suffering a severe attack of aphids (greenfly). Aphids secrete a sugary liquid known as honeydew which gently rains down on all beneath. The layer of sticky honeydew is soon colonised by a minute fungus called sooty mould. It has no direct harmful effect on leaves but is unsightly, and when dense, cuts down the amount of sunlight and therefore photosynthetic activity. No immediate cure can be effected, but in subsequent years the tree above should be sprayed in winter with a tar oil wash to kill the aphid eggs.

Leaves with spit-like frothy masses

In early summer, the wet, frothy masses known as cuckoo spit are a common sight. Quite often they are accompanied by a mild distortion of the leaf. The spit is caused by the nymphal (juvenile) stages of the jumping bug called a froghopper. Severe attacks can stunt growth and cripple stems and leaves. The soft insect is easily killed with forcible spraying of nicotine or malathion.

Leaves withering

See *Stems collapsing or withering*.

Stems collapsing or withering

Young stems with leaves can suddenly wither when in full growth. Clematis is the main sufferer, the primary cause being probably a die-back fungus, though the biology of this wilting is not fully understood. Quite often the whole plant dies, sometimes one to a few stems only. Spraying the whole plant with dinocap sometimes effects a cure.

Seedlings may wither at ground level and topple over. This is caused by damping-off disease and generally only occurs when the seedlings are overcrowded. Water the remaining seedlings with Cheshunt Compound, Captan or Zineb. Make sure to sow seeds more thinly in future.

Stems deformed

See *Leaves deformed*.

Stems with scales

Small scale-like sedentary insects sometimes appear on stems. Several kinds occur but the commonest are the brown scale, a strongly humped glossy brown insect, and mussel scale which is smaller, pale brown, flattened and narrowly pear-shaped. Both suck sap and can weaken plants if in abundance. Young scale insects are minute but very active and this is the stage at which to carry out control measures. From late spring to early summer spray at seven to ten day intervals with malathion, diazinon or nicotine. At other times of the year a systemic insecticide such as dimethoate can be tried.

In frost-free areas and under glass mealy bugs can be a nuisance. They resemble scale insects but are softer and covered with a whitish, waxy powder and filaments. Malathion provides a partial cure, but it must be brushed onto bare stems, especially when the bugs are in the axils of the branchlets or in bark crevices.

Flowers eaten

Petals, particularly of clematis and rose flowers, may be eaten. The main causes are earwigs and caterpillars. For control, see *Leaves eaten*.

Flowers withering or failing to develop

Climbers on walls in the lee of prevailing rain-bearing winds may suffer partial drought when the rest of the garden seems adequately moist. Failure of flower buds to develop properly and wilting of petals and leaves, at least on hot days, are the main symptoms. Regular watering during dry spells is the only cure.

CHAPTER 5

A-Z of
Genera and Species

Aconitum (Monkshood) *Ranunculaceae*

Although the majority of the 300 north temperate species in this genus are erect, herbaceous perennials, a select few are twining climbers. Closely related to *Delphinium* they are readily distinguished by the helmet-shaped, petal-like sepal at the top of each flower. They are excellent climbers to grow through a tallish, spring flowering shrub, providing colour and interest at a season when the shrub is rather dull. A moisture retentive, fertile soil is required in sun or partial shade and planting can take place from autumn to spring. Propagation is by seeds in spring, or as soon as ripe, or by division at planting time. The young growth in particular is very prone to slug damage and pellets should be put down every spring as a precaution.

A. bulleyanum (Zone 8) (China) is described as being 90-120 cm tall with red or blue-purple flowers. It was collected by George Forrest in the Tali (now Dali) range, Yunnan, earlier this century and almost certainly is no longer in cultivation. With the lifting of the 'bamboo curtain', however, and the first Anglo-Chinese expedition already accomplished, it might again be seen in western gardens.

A. hemsleyanum (Zone 8) (China) has heart-shaped basal leaves that become deeply three to five-lobed higher up. The comparatively large violet flowers are borne in erect racemes. Like *A. bulleyanum*, it is unlikely to be in cultivation at present, but may one day be re-introduced.

A. volubile (Zone 7) (Altai Mountains) is the only climbing monkshood to be encountered in western gardens. It is a vigorous species twining to 3-5 m in height if given the opportunity. The slender stems bear three to seven lobed or segmented deep green leaves and good sized, bright blue-purple flowers in loose, often drooping racemes. It blooms late, from August to late autumn, weather permitting, and when well suited in a sunny, sheltered site can put on a prolific show. It looks splendid rambling through a big *Escallonia* 'Edinensis', the late scattering of pink flowers contrasting attractively with those of the monkshood. Another possibility as a

A

35

host plant is a red-berrying shrub, particularly a *Berberis* or a *Cotoneaster*.

Actinidia (cat plant, Chinese gooseberry) *Actinidiaceae*

This genus of about forty deciduous, hardy, twining climbers from eastern Asia contains plants useful for foliage, flowers and fruit. *A. chinensis* is one of the very few climbing plants that are grown purely for their fruit on a commercial scale. They have lanceolate to ovate, toothed leaves and in summer, five-petalled bowl-shaped flowers in small clusters from the leaf axils. Some species are dioecious; that is, the flowers are either male or female only and carried on different plants. Rounded to oblong, edible berries follow but are not common on cultivated plants unless both sexes are present. Any fertile soil is suitable, preferably in a partially shaded, sheltered site, though *A. chinensis* is best in sun. Propagation is easiest by cuttings with a heel in late summer, ideally with bottom heat. Seeds should be sown in spring under glass. The taller actinidias look best rambling through a tree, the shorter ones are ideal for clothing walls, pergolas and tall tree stumps.

A. *arguta* (Zone 4) (China, Japan, Korea) is vigorous, easily reaching 20 m or more in a tree. It had broadly ovate, deep lustrous green leaves up to 10 cm or more long, carried on pink stalks. In the variety *A. a. cordifolia* each leaf has a conspicuous heart-shaped base. The 2 cm-wide flowers are fragrant, white, tinted with pale green. They are borne in summer in clusters of two or three. If two plants are grown, 2-3 cm long greenish-yellow fruits develop. They are eaten in Japan, but are rather tasteless to western palates. *A. arguta* is a variable species in the wild and several more or less distinct entities have been given separate species names. *A. giraldii* with broader leaves and *A. rufa* with reddish-brown hairs on flower stalks and sepals are now included within *A. arguta*.

A. *chinensis* (Zone 7) (China) was first reported to the west by Robert Fortune who saw it while collecting for the Royal Horticultural Society in 1847, but it was left to E.H. Wilson to introduce it as seeds in 1900. Although not so colourful as *A. kolomikta*, it is undoubtedly the most handsome in general appearance. Both vigorous and robust, growing to 10 m or more in length, its young stems and leaf stalks are coated with conspicuous red hairs. This red fuzz nicely sets off the bold, dark green, rounded foliage. On the long climbing stems the leaves are heart-shaped and on big specimens can be 15-20 cm long. On the short flowering shoots they are smaller, usually with notched tips. The 4 cm-wide flowers are white on opening, gradually maturing to a pleasing shade of creamy-buff. Known as Chinese gooseberries and Kiwi fruit, the berries are shortly oblong, densely covered with coarse, short, brown hair. Both sexes are needed for fruit production, through herma-phrodite plants are known. Although grown in plantations here and there in the temperate world, New Zealand has very much made it its own and a considerable quantity is exported to Britain under the now more familiar name of Kiwi fruit. A plantation I visited in North Island some years ago was growing them on wire fences with one male to several females at intervals. Three cultivars were in use, 'Monty's', 'Abbots' and 'Hayward's', all differing slightly in flavour, the latter with a smaller crop of larger fruits. The berries should be kept for at least a month after harvesting to develop their full flavour. To encourage flowering and fruiting the young shoots are regularly pinched back to about 30 cm throughout the summer. In winter, the long spurs are further shortened.

A. coriacea (*A. henryi*) (Zone 7) (China) produces stems 6-8 m in length clad with slender pointed, rather narrow leaves 7-14 cm long. Each leaf blade is smooth and leathery, deep green above, paler beneath. The fragrant flowers are smallish, about 12 mm wide, varying from rose-pink to red with pale green sepals. They may be borne singly or in clusters of two to four. The 2 cm-long egg-shaped, brown berries are white dotted, but seldom seen in cultivation. In Britain this distinctive actinidia is not fully hardy, needing longer, warmer summers to ripen the growth satisfactorily. It is, in fact, native to the fairly southerly latitudes of Szechwan. E.H. Wilson collected it in Mupin and on Mt Omei, introducing it in 1908.

A. henryi (China) has been mistakenly used for *A. coriacea*. The true species with ovate leaves and white flowers is probably no longer in cultivation.

A. kolomikta (Zone 4) (China, Korea, Japan) tends to be a rather bushy, slender climber in gardens, usually under 3-4 m in height and only rarely to 6 m. In the wild, however, it is a very different plant being much more vigorous and sometimes in such abundance as to make large areas of woodland virtually impenetrable. It is one of the few temperate zone plants which has naturally variegated leaves, a characteristic more common in the tropics or among mutant garden plants. It has ovate to oblong leaves, usually heart-shaped at the base and 7-15 cm long, carried on downy stalks. In shade they are mainly plain green. Where sunlight strikes them for at least part of the day, anything from the extreme tips to the whole leaves turn white with a pink flush. A well coloured plant in summer presents a most striking sight equal to or exceeding the floral display of many a more popular plant. Later in the season, the colours fade. There is some evidence to show that male plants colour better than female ones. Certainly male plants are more commonly met with in gardens. The flowers are fragrant, smallish and white and rather hidden by the leaves. Not unnaturally, the small, pleasantly flavoured gooseberry-like yellowish fruits are seldom seen. *Actinidia kolomikta* is one of that select band of plants that excites cats in a curiously unreasoning way. In France it is known as *herbe aux chats*, and sometimes in this country as cat plant. The nibbling and frantic rubbing activities of some cats (not all are so affected) can injure a young plant or even kill it unless protected with wire netting.

A. melanandra (Zone 5) (China) in the wild of Hupeh and Szechwan soars up into tall trees, and in cultivation grows with some vigour. It has smaller leaves than most cultivated species having lance-shaped blades borne on decorative, long pink stalks and white, 2 cm-wide unisexual flowers. The egg-shaped, 2-3 cm long fruits are brown but with a waxy white patina. This is a neglected species seldom now commercially available. Although not one of the most outstanding, it does have its merits, not least being the blue-white leaf undersides which are displayed decoratively whenever the wind is stronger than a light breeze.

A. polygama (Zone 4) (China, Korea, Japan) is known as the silver vine for its silvery-white (sometimes yellowish) variegated leaves in the style of *A. kolomikta*. It is, in fact, allied to and confused with that species and has the same attraction for cats. It is, however, a somewhat more vigorous species, with leaf blades that are rounded or tapered to their bristly-hairy stalks. The fruits too differ, being beaked or bottle-shaped translucent yellow and less pleasantly flavoured. Plants in cultivation with variegated leaves are invariably male; female plants appear to be usually green only.

A. purpurea (Zone 6) (China) seldom occurs outside botanic gardens. It is closely allied to the variable *A. arguta* but can be easily distinguished by its elliptic leaves, smaller, 1.5 cm-wide flowers and purple fruits. The latter are described as sweet and pleasantly flavoured but, regrettably, are rarely produced in cultivation.

Adlumia (climbing fumitory) *Fumariaceae*

This genus contains two biennials, one from eastern USA, the other from Korea. They have fern-like dissected leaves which cling to their supports in the same way as clematis, and drooping clusters of curious tubular flowers like slender hearts. They need a site sheltered from wind and a moisture retentive soil to thrive really well, but are not difficult to grow. Seed is the only means of propagation and, ideally, should be sown as soon as ripe. The seedlings should be pricked off singly into pots, or directly into the flowering site. Root damage at a later stage can result in small plants lacking in vigour. First year plants form elegant rosettes, climbing stems being produced only in the second year. A batch of plants from seed sown early under glass does, however, often produce one or two individuals that elongate in late summer or early autumn and produce a few flowers. These are best discarded. This is a plant that looks best scrambling up a tall shrub; a wall-trained pyracantha is ideal. Pot grown plants should be set out as soon as they have about a half dozen leaves.

A. fungosa (Zone 8) (eastern USA) is the only species cultivated. Also known as mountain fringe, it has slender stems to 4 m or so tall and quite large leaves formed of small, pale green, lobed leaflets. The spongy-petalled flowers are basically white, variably flushed pink, pale purple or green and open in sizeable panicles from summer to autumn. This is a perfect plant for those fortunate enough to garden in a wood.

Akebia (chocolate vine) *Lardizabalaceae*

Eastern Asia is the home territory of the five twining climbers in this genus. They are deciduous or semi-evergreen with compound leaves composed of three or five radiating leaflets. The flowers are borne in pendent racemes from the axils of the first leaves to expand in spring. Each raceme has one to three large basal female flowers and several much smaller males beyond. In favourable years there is a bonus of livid-purple, fleshy, sausage-like fruits of unique appearance. Any fertile soil is suitable, even chalky ones. Propagation is easily carried out by layering, hard or semi-hardwood cuttings. Seeds can be sown when ripe or in spring.

A. quinata (Zone 4) (China, Korea, Japan) is the most vigorous and decorative species, soon weaving a substantial tapestry of slender stems and rich green pentafoliate leaves. When well established it can rise to 12 m or more in a tree. In mild winters it is semi- to almost evergreen; in cold ones it is completely deciduous. In spring the young leaves are purple flushed and among them, the small strings of pale flower buds show up promisingly. By late spring these buds have become fragrant, chocolate to maroon-purple flowers, the females 2-3 cm wide and darker than the males. A well flowered specimen can be quite showy and is sure to excite comment. The greyish-purple fruits are up to 10 cm long and are decidedly intriguing objects, particularly when on ripening they split down one side to reveal white pulp in which are imbedded black seeds.

A trifoliata (*A. lobata*) (Zone 5) (Japan) is equally vigorous and fully deciduous. The trifoliate leaves are composed of rather larger leaflets than those of *A. quinata* and are slightly lustrous. Flowering takes place at the same time and the blossoms are much like those of the preceding species except that the male flowers are even smaller, about 4 mm wide as against 6 mm of *A. quinata*. The fruits are larger, up to 13 cm long by 4-6 cm wide and even more striking in appearance. When the two species are growing together as they may, both in the wild and in gardens, they cross readily. Hybrid

39

plants were first detected in the wild and subsequently named *A*. X *pentaphylla*. They are halfway between the species with mainly five leaflets, though trifoliate leaves also occur.

Allamanda Golden trumpet (*Apocynaceae*)

None of the 15 species in this largely tropical American genus are true climbers, as they have no means of holding on. *A. cathartica* (Zone 9-10) (Brazil) is essentially a scrambler, producing long, robust but pliable stems to 10 m or more, which push up through shrubs and trees. It has narrowly elliptic leaves 10-15 cm long which are usually borne in whorls of three or four at each node. The rich yellow flowers are trumpet-shaped with five rounded, spreading petal lobes. On well grown plants flowers are 10-13 cm wide and carried in showy terminal clusters during the summer and autumn. Not infrequently, one or two of the intriguing, spine-clad, burr-like seed pods will follow. *Allamanda cathartica* is a variable plant and several fine forms or cultivars represent it in cultivation. The best of three is probably *A. c.* 'Hendersonii', having long, glossy leaves and a succession of orange-yellow blooms. *A. c.* 'Grandiflora' is also free-flowering, but carries pale yellow flowers and is not quite such a good doer. 'Schottii' is vigorous and easily distinguished by the rich brown stripes that run down the throat of each deep yellow bloom. In all zones less than 10, this is a greenhouse plant. To thrive and survive it must have an average winter minimum of 13°C and a sunny site. A large pot or small tub, rather than a ground-level bed will help to restrict both root and top growth where greenhouse room is at a premium. All the main stems need tying in as they grow but the floral display is more effective if the flowering shoots arch or hang down. Propagation is by cuttings in spring or summer at not less than 24°C.

Ampelopsis *Vitidaceae*

Most of the 20 members of this Asian and North American genus were originally classified along with the grape-vine in the genus *Vitis*. Unlike *Vitis*, however, *Ampelopsis* opens its five small petals; *Vitis* sheds them fused together like a small cap. Both climb by twining stem tendrils. The species described here are effective, deciduous foliage plants and in the sunnier, milder areas produce a crop of blue, orange, red or black fruits. The leaves may be simple and palmate or pinnate, sometimes further dissected. They grow in any fertile soil and are best in sheltered sites. The larger sorts look well cascading down from trees or tall stumps and they make decorative pergola and wall cover. Propagation is by late summer cuttings in a propagating case.

    A. aconitifolia (*Vitis aconitifolia*) (Zone 4) (China) is the most elegant species with digitate leaves composed of five lanceolate, deeply lobed, glossy, rich green leaflets creating an almost frothy effect *en masse*. The tiny greenish flowers open in late summer and are followed by pea-sized orange or yellow fruits. In the past at least there has been some confusion with *A. japonica* q.v.

A. bodinieri (Zone 5) (China) is a slender climber to 6 m, the stems of which are purple hued in a sunny site. It has undivided, broadly triangular to ovate leaves, 6-13 cm long, which are richly lustrous green above, bluish-grey beneath. On vigorous growth, some leaves are three-lobed. The flowers are carried in crowded clusters and the oblate, pea-sized fruits are deep blue. It was introduced by E.H. Wilson as long ago as 1900, but despite its handsome foliage has never become widely known and is now difficult to obtain. It deserves a better fate.

A. brevipedunculata (Zone 4) (NE Asia) has a satisfying vigour and lushness of growth and can clothe a wall or pergola to perfection. It has coarsely hairy young stems and three- to five-lobed leaves which are similarly hairy beneath. Although darker green they are of similar size and appearance as those of common hop (*Humulus*). The glory of this plant is its bright blue fruits but it needs a sunny warm wall to produce them. *A. brevipedunculata* is variable and largely represented in gardens by several selected cultivars. *A. b. maximowiczii* (*Vitis heterophylla maximowiczii*) differs only in its lack of bristly hairs and greater variety of leaf size and lobing; some leaves are unlobed. It grows mixed with the species in the wilds of China, Korea, Japan and eastern USSR and is probably no more than part of the natural variability of the species. *A. b.* 'Citrulloides' has consistently deeply five-lobed leaves, making it a more appealing foliage plant. *A. b.* 'Elegans' ('Variegata', 'Tricolor') is much weaker growing and rather frost tender. Its claim to fame is the white and pink mottled, rather smaller, somewhat distorted leaves. As *A. heterophylla* 'Variegata' it is often grown as a pot plant being called 'coloured grape leaf'. There are much better variegated climbers for the garden, notably *Actinidia kolomikta* and *Lonicera japonica* 'Aureoreticulata'.

A. chaffanjonii (*A. watsoniana*) (Zone 7) (China) departs from the norm of members of the grape family in having pinnate leaves. These can be up to 30 cm long, composed of five to seven oval leaflets which are rich glossy green above and purple suffused beneath. They usually colour red and yellow before falling in autumn. It needs a fairly rich soil and a sheltered, sunny site to succeed, and is then a most distinctive and handsome foliage plant. The small red, passing to black, berries are seldom very conspicuous, if indeed they form at all. It is not a very strong growing species, 3-5 m being an average height. Introduced in 1900 this is another of E.H. Wilson's introductions while working for the nursery firm of Veitch. It was wrongly identified as *A. leeoides* and distributed under that name for a while. True *A. leeoides* has bipinnate leaves, is a native of Japan and Taiwan and is probably not in cultivation. *A. japonica* has, at least in the past, been confused with *A. aconitifolia*, but has pinnate leaflets, pale yellow flowers and purple-blue fruits. It is a native of China and Taiwan and cultivated for medicinal purposes in Japan.

A. megalophylla (Zone 6) (China) has the distinction of bearing the longest leaves of any hardy climber. On well grown plants they are 45-60 cm long. Each one is bipinnately dissected, the ovate, toothed leaflets rich green above, glaucous beneath. The sparsely-produced late summer flowers give way to small, black fruits. Although strong growing to about 9 m in height this ampelopsis is not fast growing. It can be used to great effect as a wall cover or trained over an arbour.

A. orientalis (Zone 6) (Western Turkey, Syria) is often more of a big, loose bush than a climber. In rich soil, however, it can climb a few metres especially if first trained as a wall shrub. The leaves are rather variable, usually biternate (three sets of three leaflets), but can be partially bipinnate or even simply pinnate. Each leaflet is 3-8 cm long, ovate to diamond-shaped, coarsely toothed, deep matt green above and greyish-green beneath. The four-petalled flowers are carried in long-stalked clusters and followed by showy fruits likened to red currants.

A. sempervirens, see *Cissus striata*.

A. veitchii, see *Parthenocissus tricuspidata*.

Anredera Madeira vine *Basellaceae*

Between five and ten species are recognised in this genus of tropical American twining climbers. One only is widely cultivated in warm countries and is occasionally seen in cooler-climate greenhouses. This is *A. cordifolia* (Zone 9), more familiarly known under its synonym *Boussingaultia baselloides*, from N Argentina to S Brazil. It has a tuberous root and semi-woody reddish stems to 6 m or more clad with somewhat fleshy-textured oval to lance-shaped leaves, sometimes with heart-shaped bases. Tiny white, fragrant flowers appear in 5-10 cm long clusters from the upper leaf axils in autumn. An interesting feature is the small aerial tubers which form in the non-flowering leaf axils, and which are a ready means of propagation. Also known as mignonette vine, from the scent of the flowers, it is a vigorous plant in a border or a large tub of humus-rich, well-drained soil. In smaller containers it is more constrained and can be trained under the greenhouse roof to provide summer shade for things below. In warm countries it grows most of the year and is a useful screening plant. In cooler climates it either stops growing in winter,

42

or is killed back to ground level. If the site it occupies is mounded over with coarse sand or gravel in late autumn it can even be grown in zones 7-8. Although invariably seen as a climber, without support it makes a luxuriant ground cover for wild areas. I well remember once some years ago when exploring one of the less frequented parts of Pascua (Easter Island), coming across a vast mound of its exuberant greenery covering a ruined ahu (platform on which formerly stood some of the famed stone statues). Not only did it tell that here was a site of former human occupation, but it was a most welcome sight in a rocky, rather desolate and treeless landscape.

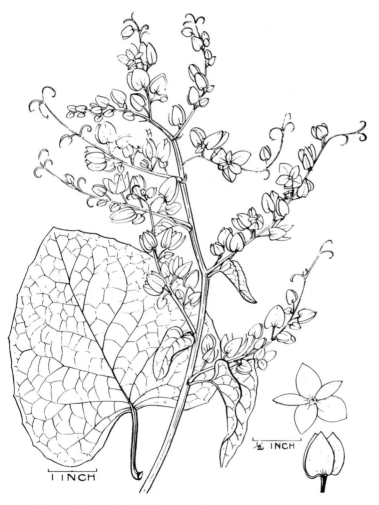

Figure 5.1
Antigonon leptopus,
the coral vine

Antigonon (Coral vine) *Polygonaceae*

Depending upon the botanical authority, there are between two and eight species in this tropical and sub-tropical genus from the Americas.

43

Only one is well known, *A. leptopus* (Zone 9) from Mexico. This is a slender, but very vigorous, plant growing to 12 m or so with broadly to narrowly ovate leaves having a wide, heart-shaped base. On strong young stems they can exceed 12 cm in length but are usually less. Although evergreen and perennial, it has a tuberous root and if the top is destroyed it quickly re-grows. In its native country its edible tubers are esteemed for their nut-like flavour, but whether raw or cooked I have been unable to find out. In tropical countries or during the warm season of cooler ones, it grows with great speed, flowering the whole time. The method of clinging to its support is intriguing; small hooked tendrils terminate the branches of the flower cluster. The usual flower colour is bright pink and this is carried in the five spreading sepals; there are no petals. Each flower, which is about 2 cm wide, is composed of three broad and two narrow sepals. The flowers are usually borne in racemes from the leaf axils but may also occur in terminal panicles. In either case, tendrils are present. *A. l.* 'Album' has white flowers and forms are known which vary in shades of pink to deep red. Double-flowered forms are also grown. After flowering, the sepals increase in size, sheltering the angular, nut-like fruit. The popularity of this climber is echoed in its many vernacular names, e.g. Corallita, Confederate vine, Love vine, Chain-of-love, Mountain rose, Queen's jewels, Queen's wreath. It is a good bee plant. In the zones below 10, antigonon needs greenhouse culture or a winter minimum of 10°C. It is best in a ground level bed and needs plenty of sun to flower well. In Britain, although it grows well, it flowers rather sparingly. Propagation is by cuttings or seeds in summer.

Apios (Groundnut) *Leguminosae*

Of the eight to ten species in this genus, only one is sometimes cultivated, *A. americana* (Zone 3) (*A. tuberosa*, *Glycine apios*) from eastern North America. Also known as potato bean, this hardy herbaceous perennial has more of interest than beauty though it is by no means entirely lacking in the latter. It is a slender twiner 1-1.5 m tall with pinnate leaves composed of five ovate, slender-pointed leaflets. The pea-like flowers open in late summer and are maroon and fawn-tinted lilac with a sweet, somewhat cloying fragrance reminiscent of violets. Each flower is about 12 mm long and several together form dense spike-like clusters on stalks from the leaf axils. Although basically pea-shaped the flowers are of curious construction having somewhat tubular, coiled keel petals. J.C. Willis in his *A Dictionary of Flowering Plants and Ferns* (only in editions one to six) says: 'The keel of the flower forms a tube which bends up and rests against a depression in the standard (petal). When liberated by insects the tension of the keel makes it spring downwards, coiling up more closely, and causing the essential organs (stigma and stamens) to emerge at the apex'. The long-lived root stock is formed of chains of small, edible tubers, formerly part of the diet of the local Indians. Early settlers from Europe and particularly members of the (second) colonising expedition led by Sir Richard Grenville in 1585 to Roanoke Island, Virginia, relied on them when other foods failed. As a result of their introduction to Britain at the same time as tubers of the true potato (*Solanum tuberosum*) from South America the history of the two for a time became entwined and confused; see *The History and Social Influence of the Potato* by R.N. Salaman (1949) pp. 80-84.

Araujia (Cruel plant) *Asclepiadaceae*

Only one of the two to three known species in this S. American genus is cultivated. This is *A. sericofera* (Zone 8-9) from southern S. America, an evergreen twiner growing to 7 m or more. (*Araujia* is the Brazilian vernacular name in Latin form). Also known as moth plant, white bladder-flower and kapok-plant, it has 5-10 cm long oblong-ovate pale green leaves in pairs. Both leaf undersides and stems are thinly felted. During late summer, 2.5-3 cm wide, shortly tubular, white flowers open in loose, stalked clusters from the upper leaf axils. They are fragrant and visited by night flying moths. The latter are sometimes held temporarily by their tongues to the sticky, waxy pollen. After the flowers have been pollinated, large pods rather like grooved ridge cucumbers develop, sometimes exceeding 12 cm in length. They are seldom freely produced, but individual plants vary in their fruiting capabilities. When ripe, the pods split to release the many flattened seeds, each with its parachute of long, silky hairs. Except for the very mildest areas, that is in all zones less than 9, this plant needs greenhouse protection and a minimum winter temperature of 7°-10°C. It thrives in large pots of any proprietary compost and needs plenty of sun to flower well. Propagation is by seed in spring, or late summer cuttings, both at not less than 18°-20°C.

Aristolochia (Birthwort) *Aristolochiaceae*

Primarily of tropical origins, there are no less than 300 species in this genus spread around the world on both sides of the equator. They are mainly woody, climbing twiners, both evergreen and deciduous, with a few herbaceous perennials. Both sorts have large, fleshy, underground roots or rhizomes. The flowers have a unique structure lacking both recognisable sepals and petals. These organs appear to be fused into a single curved or bent tube, the basal part being more or less inflated, surrounding the sex organs of the flower. Above this inflated part is a short, narrow tube the top of which dilates rapidly

45

Figure 5.2
Araujia sericofera,
the cruel plant

1 INCH

1 INCH

into a wide variety of bizarre forms. Within the tube are numerous downwards-pointing hairs screening the way to the pistil and stamens. Small flies pollinate the flowers attracted by the malodorous scent. They easily push by the hinged hairs, but are unable to force their way out again. The basal part of the flower is then an efficient insect trap in the same style as that of the arums. Soon, the stamens shed their pollen onto the flies and the hairs wither. The flies, gluttons for punishment, visit another flower and pollen from their bodies is rubbed off on the stigma, effecting pollination. The stamens shed their pollen and the cycle is repeated. After pollination a cylindrical to ovoid pendent seed capsule forms, strengthened by six tough, longitudinal ribs. When ripe, the capsule splits from the base down between the ribs creating an intriguing basket-like object. By a combination of wind and the contraction of the ribs, the smallish, flattened seeds are flung far and wide. In zones below 9, most climbing species need greenhouse protection. They grow well in large pots or tubs of a proprietary compost and will flower even in quite shady conditions. Propagation is by seed in spring or cuttings in summer with bottom heat at not less than 21°-23°C.

A. altissima, see *A. sempervirens*.

A. chrysops (Zone 8) (China) has yellow hairy stems growing to 6 m long and ovate leaves with prominent lobes at the base. The flowers are about 4 cm long rather like a truncated saxophone, the expanded mouth being maroon with a contrasting yellow throat. They expand on dangling stalks in early summer. It is a rare species now hard to find in British gardens, but may well be re-introduced now that its Chinese homeland — from whence it was brought by E.H. Wilson in 1904 — is again open to western botanists.

A. durior, see *A. macrophylla*.

A. elegans (Zone 9-10) (calico flower) (Brazil) is a vigorous, slender climber growing to 7 m or so with heart or kidney-shaped leaves to 8 cm wide. Throughout the summer it produces a succession of long-stalked dangling flowers, the mouths of which are like 12 cm wide shallow, heart-shaped bowls of rich maroon with white marbling. Of the tender species it is the most decorative and least bizarre, and additionally lacks the unpleasant smell of most species. It needs a winter temperature of 10°-12°C, but will survive short spells at 7°C if kept dry.

A. griffithii (Nepal) needs to be kept more or less frost-free to thrive. It can climb to 6 m or more, its slender stems clad with heart-shaped leaves to 10 cm wide. In early summer it produces euphonium-shaped flowers, the expanded mouth to 7 cm wide, dark red, and intriguingly papillose. The tubular part is strongly curved and white without. Like *A. chrysops* it is rare in cultivation but due for re-introduction.

47

A. heterophylla (Zone 6) (China) is related to *A. chrysops*, being a deciduous, more or less hardy species but with larger heart-shaped leaves and slightly smaller, bright yellow and brown-purple flowers.

A. macrophylla (Zone 4) (*A. durior, A. sipho*) (eastern USA) is the original Dutchman's pipe, introduced to Britain as long ago as 1783. It is essentially a foliage plant and a handsome one at that, with long-stalked, light green, kidney to heart-shaped leaves up to 25 cm or more long. The small flowers, 2.5-4 cm long, have U-shaped yellow-green tubes and brown-purple three-lobed mouths. They appear in summer and are often more or less obscured by the young leaves. Deciduous and hardy, this Dutchman's pipe is a good doer in gardens, growing vigorously to 8 m or more. It makes a fine pergola plant and can cover a wall most effectively.

A. sempervirens (Zone 8-9) (*A. altissima*) (SE Europe, N Africa) is often grown as a free-standing, shrub-like tangle, but given support it makes a pleasing, small evergreen climber 2-3 m in height. The leafage is dark and lustrous, each blade being roughly heart-shaped and pointed, 5 cm or more in length. From early to late summer, 2.5-4 cm long tubular flowers appear, each one with a funnel-shaped mouth and one large lobe. Formerly, *A. altissima* and *A. sempervirens* were considered to be separate species, the latter being somewhat smaller, having purplish flowers and being confined to the island of Crete. Further botanical exploration, however, revealed a complete gradation of forms linking *sempervirens* with the larger, yellow-brown flowered *altissima* and the two were united under the oldest — first published — name.

A. tomentosa (Zone 5) (south-eastern USA) resembles and is related to *A. macrophylla* but has downy hairy or woolly stems, young leaves and flowers. The latter also have yellow-flared mouths and the mature leaves are somewhat smaller.

Asarina *Scrophulariaceae*

This genus of 16 species is allied to the snapdragons (*Antirrhinum*) and has similar, but open-mouthed, tubular flowers with five broad petal lobes. The leaves, however, are alternate, triangular to ovate and carried on trailing to climbing stems. In the climbing species the leaf stalks act as tendrils. Mexico is the main country of origin with some species in western USA and one — the rock garden trailer, *A. procumbens* (*Antirrhinum asarina*) — in the Pyrenees. The climbing species described here are half-hardy perennials and need greenhouse conditions in zones below 8. They will, however, flower the first year if the seed is sown early under glass, and can be treated like half-hardy annuals. Propagation is by seeds sown at 18°C, or basal cuttings from established plants in late spring. Any well-drained fertile soil in sun or partial shade, sheltered from strong winds, is suitable for culture outdoors.

A. antirrhiniflora (Zone 8-9) (*Maurandya antirrhiniflora*, *Antirrhinum maurandioides*) has very slender stems 1-2 m long or sometimes more under greenhouse conditions. The halberd-shaped leaves are 1-3 cm long and from their upper axils spring violet-purple flowers 2.5 cm or more in length. The slenderness of the stems and smallness of the leaves and flowers gives this little climber a delicacy and charm which sets it apart from its fellows. Astonishingly enough, it inhabits rather hot, arid regions, usually on limestone, including the Mohave Desert. Often it has no opportunity to climb, and trails down cliffs and rocky slopes in shade. Some years ago when walking the Bright Angel Trail down near the bottom of the Grand Canyon and not too far from the Colorado River, I happened upon a plant hanging at head height almost above the trail. Having no idea that this *Asarina* was native there my surprise was the more complete to find so delicate seeming a plant in such an arid, hostile environment.

A. barclaiana (Zone 8-9) (*Maurandya barclaiana*) (Mexico) is a woody-based species 2-5 m in height, having roughly triangular leaf blades mounted on long stalks. The flowers are 3-5 cm long and vary from white and pink to deep purple. This species quite often masquerades as *A. scandens* (q.v.).

A. erubescens (Zone 8-9) (creeping gloxinia) (*Maurandya erubescens*) is native to Mexico. The whole plant is sticky, glandular-hairy with grey-green, toothed leaves which are more or less triangular in outline. The flowers are relatively large, 5-7.5 cm long, rose-pink, each one sitting in a broad, almost leafy-lobed calyx. This is perhaps the showiest of the cultivated species and makes a fine cool greenhouse plant.

A scandens (Zone 8-9) (*Maurandya scandens*) (Mexico) is similar to *A. barclaiana*, a species with which it is confused in gardens. Usually the flower colour proclaims the true species, as *scandens* is normally lavender. The calyx lobes differ also, being smooth and devoid of hairs, whereas *barclaiana* has glandular down on the sepal lobes.

Asparagus (asparagus fern) *Liliaceae*

Depending on the botanical authority there are between 100 and 300 species in this genus spread over Europe and Asia and south into Africa. All are perennials, often with tuberous roots and more or less woody stems. Some are erect or spreading, others twine and climb. Their primary distinctive character is a lack of foliage. What appear to be leaves are technically phylloclades, small, often flattened stems with the form and function of true leaves. The flowers are tiny, with six white or green tepals and give way to red or black berries. A sheltered, sunny site and well-drained soil are their basic requirements. Tender species grow well in pots of any proprietary compost. Propagation is by division or seeds in spring.

Figure 5.3
Asarina barclaiana

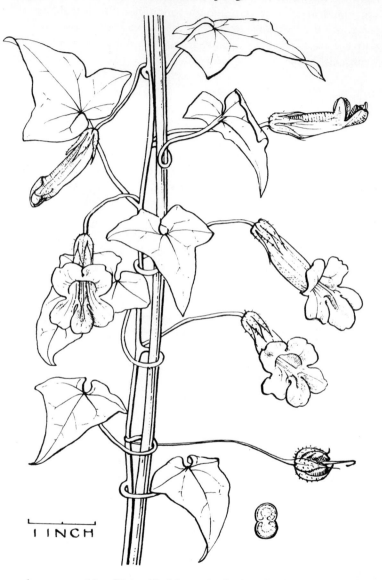

I INCH

A. asparagoides (Zone 9) (*A. medeoloides, Smilax asparagoides*) (South Africa) is the 'smilax' of florists but should not be confused with the true members of the *Smilax* genus. When established it can climb rapidly to 3 m or more, the numerous side branches clad with glossy, bright green, very leaf-like ovate phylloclades up to 3 cm

50

long. The greenish-white flowers are insignificant but are sometimes followed by red berries which contrast pleasingly with the handsome leafage.

A. plumosus, see next entry.

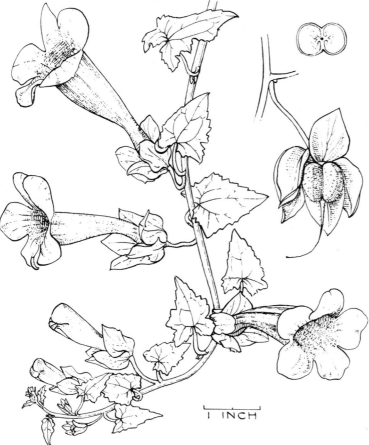

Figure 5.4
Asarina erubescens

⊢ INCH ⊣

A. setaceus (Zone 9) (*A. plumosus*) (S Africa) is the popular asparagus fern so much in demand by florists for making up button-holes and bouquets. It starts life as a bushy, erect plant with much branched, frond-like stems clad with numerous bristle-like deep green phylloclades. The overall effect is astonishingly fern-like and extremely elegant. If regularly potted on or grown in a bed of good soil, after two or more years, strong, twining stems appear which, in time, can reach 3 m or so. These produce the frond-like branches alternately and horizontally for most of their length. The tiny white flowers and purple-black berries are not a noteworthy feature. The readily available pot plants of this asparagus are usually of *A. s.* 'Nanus' which never, or only very rarely, produces climbing stems.

A. verticillatus (Zone 6-7) (Southern USSR to Iran) ascends

51

3-5 m on stems which eventually get quite woody. The slender side branches bear sharp prickles and myriads of 1.5-5 cm long hair-like phylloclades arranged in clusters of three to ten. Tiny funnel-shaped flowers give rise to red pea-sized berries. Seldom seen, this hardy species deserves to be grown more often. It makes an interesting background framework for a lesser climber to unite with, for example *Clematis afoliata* or *Bomarea edulis*.

Asteranthera *Gesneriaceae*

Only one species represents this southern S American genus and it is in every way a star turn. *Asteranthera* is derived from the Latin *aster*, a star, and *anthera*, anther, alluding to the joined anthers which fancifully resemble a shooting star. In its homeland of Chile and Argentina *A. ovata* (Zone 8-9) is often called *estrellita del bosque* which I freely translate as little star of the woods. In this case the name refers to its glowing, red flowers which do seem almost to shine from the shady recesses of the temperate rain forests it inhabits. It is a self-clinging evergreen climber growing to 5 m, holding on firmly by its aerial roots. The leaves are small — 6-20 mm long — broadly ovate, toothed, and carried in opposite pairs. They form a rich green clothing over tree trunks and walls against which the flowers are backgrounded with startling effect. Each flower has a 2.5-3 cm long tube and four oblong-oval petal lobes with a total spread of 4-4.5 cm. The overall effect is of a greenhouse *Columnea* and indeed it was at one time included in that more tropical genus. In the wild it creeps about like ivy, covering the soil and fallen tree trunks until it meets with something substantial and erect. I have vivid memories of seeing a particularly vigorous specimen climbing up the smooth, grey bole of a southern beech (*Nothofagus*) in southern Chile, looking for all the world like a tongue of flame. In all zones below 8 it is a cool greenhouse plant and even in zone 8 it needs a really sheltered site. There is a superb mass of it beside a shady north wall at Nymans Gardens in Sussex, brought back by the horticulturist and plant collector Harold Comber in the 1920s and whose father was head gardener there at the time. Although cut back from time to time by hard winters, it always survives. It needs little in the way of soil, thriving best in leaf mould with a little bone meal. Whatever the rooting medium it should be neutral to acid; in pots, an all peat rhododendron mix is ideal.

B

Beaumontia (herald's trumpet) *Apocynaceae*

About 15 species form this far eastern genus. Only one, *B. grandiflora* (Zone 9) from northern India, is widely grown. It is a stem twiner 3-6 m tall with large, handsome, lustrous, ovate-oblong leaves and 13-20 cm long fragrant, white trumpet-shaped blossoms in terminal trusses. The young shoots are attractively rusty-hairy. In sub-tropical gardens it is used to spectacular effect climbing through and over quite large trees. Where the summers are warm and moist it grows with great vigour and can easily reach the top of a 15 m tree, there arching downwards to create a show-stopping display of its huge white flowers. In zones less than 9 it requires cool greenhouse conditions, the plant kept at 7°-10°C during the winter and on the dry side to initiate flowering in the following spring or early summer. It succeeds in pots of all peat compost and can be kept to size by pruning immediately after flowering. Later pruning will curtail the following season's flowering. *B. jerdoniana* from S. India is probably no more than a form or variety of *grandiflora* differing only in very small botanical features. Most obvious are the red flower buds, the more abruptly expanded flower tube and the almost smooth leaf undersurfaces; those of *grandiflora* are red-brown hairy.

Berberidopsis *Flacourtiaceae*

Like *Asteranthera* and *Lapageria*, this is another genus from S America containing one exceptionally garden-worthy species. *B. corallina* (Zone 8-9) is native to mid-Chile where it is either very rare or already extinct. Happily it is well established in cultivation, at least in Britain and New Zealand where it grows outside in sheltered sites and also makes a fine specimen for a shaded, frost-free greenhouse. It is an evergreen twiner with stems 2-3 m long clad in semi-lustrous, rich green foliage. The leaves are 5-10 cm long, oblong-ovate with a squared to heart-shaped base and finely pointed, almost spiny teeth. It is the sort of foliage which makes a perfect background for the pendent trusses of crimson, almost globular flowers which open during the summer and autumn. Superficially, the flowers resemble those of barberry (*Berberis*) hence the generic name, but are larger — about 1 cm wide — and composed of nine to fifteen tepals. The fruit is a many seeded berry but seldom seen on cultivated plants. Neutral to acid, humus-rich soil and a partially shaded, sheltered site are the key points of successful cultivation. Under such conditions it will put up with short spells of drought with ease. Propagation is surprisingly easy from cuttings at almost any time of the year providing bottom heat of about 15°-18°C can be maintained; the autumn to winter period is the best time.

Berchemia *Rhamnaceae*

Allied to buckthorn (*Rhamnus*) and Christ's thorn (*Paliurus*), there are about 20 species in this little-cultivated genus of woody twiners from Asia, Africa, N and S America. About five of the hardy species have been introduced, three of which are sometimes available. All of these have simple, deciduous leaves, clusters of small white or green flowers and red to blue-black fruits. They thrive in ordinary soil but do not relish dry conditions. A sunny site is best but light shade is tolerated. Propagation is by late summer cuttings under glass.

B. giraldiana (Zone 7) (China) is more of a scrambler than a true climber but can still achieve 6 m or so in a tree. It is one of the most elegant in habit, with oval to rounded leaves pleasingly disposed on the arching and hanging side stems. Each leaf is up to 6 cm long with a light bluish-green patina above and more strongly glaucous beneath. The young shoots are a glowing reddish-brown and the small white flowers are carried in terminal panicles up to 20 cm in length. They are followed by small, cylindrical fruits that change from green to red and finally black. It was discovered by the Italian missionary Guiseppe Giraldi during the 1890s but did not reach Britain (Kew) until almost 20 years later, via Les Barres, France.

B. lineata (N India, China, Taiwan) twines its way up to 3 m or more on slender, downy stems. The elliptic leaves are neatly and distinctly parallel-veined, varying greatly in length from as little as 6 mm to a maximum 4 cm. Although smallish as leaves go, they are borne in abundance and give a plumy effect to the arching growths. The flowers are white in both terminal and lateral clusters on the side stems. The oval to short-cylindrical fruits ripen blue-black and are quite decorative.

B. racemosa (Zone 7) (Japan) is the best known species, a vigorous scrambler and twiner growing to 5 m, though it is, like *B. giraldiana*, more likely to form a bushy tangle unless directed and trained on its upward journey. The leaves are narrowly heart-shaped, to about 7 cm long and with a light blue-white patina beneath. They turn yellow in autumn. Tiny greenish flowers open in tapered, terminal panicles in late summer and give way to oblong-ovoid fruits which change from red to black. Although it grows well in Britain it seldom fruits with any abundance. Where summers are sunnier and generally warmer it fruits abundantly and is then very ornamental. For those who enjoy variegated plants, the cream-patterned leaf form *B. r.* 'Variegata' is worth seeking out.

Bignonia *Bignoniaceae*

Although formerly a genus of about 150 species, only one now remains, the rest having been re-classified into several other genera, e.g. *Campsis, Doxantha, Clytostoma, Pandorea, Pyrostegia* and *Tecomaria*. The lone survivor is *Bignonia capreolata* (Zone 8) (*Doxantha capreolata*) from the south-eastern USA. Known colloquially as cross vine — from the pattern revealed when the stem is cut through — it is a very vigorous evergreen species capable of reaching the tops of 12-15 m tall trees. It climbs by means of slender tendrils. Each leaf is composed of two, narrowly ovate to lance-shaped leaflets, 5-10 cm long. Between them, and growing as a continuation of the leaf stalk, is a branched tendril doubtless evolved from one to several leaflets. The tips of the tendrils may bear hooks or adhesive discs. Around mid-summer, 4-5 cm long foxglove-like flowers open in clusters from the upper leaf axils. They are orange-red in colour, rather paler within. The cross vine is fairly hardy in southern England, though often only semi-evergreen and seldom flowering abundantly. Nevertheless it makes a fine cover for a warm wall. In general it thrives best in zones 9 and 10. It is more highly esteemed in S Africa, Australia and the North Island of New Zealand. It does well in most ordinary soils that stay reasonably moist, and can be propagated by seed or stem cuttings in spring in a frame with bottom heat 21°-24°C.

Billardiera Apple-berry *Pittosporaceae*

Whether there are 6 or 9 species in this genus — botanical reference works seem undecided — all are native to Australia, Tasmania included. They are small, slender twiners with mainly narrow leaves, five-petalled, bell-shaped nodding flowers and berry-like edible fruits often strikingly coloured. They need humus-rich, neutral to acid soil and thrive in sun or partial shade. Outside the milder parts of zone 8 this genus needs greenhouse treatment with enough heat only to keep out frost. Propagation is by seeds in spring or cuttings in late summer with a bottom heat of 18°-20°C.

B. longifolia (Zone 8-9) (SE Australia, Tasmania) climbs to 2 m or more and looks charming rambling through a wall shrub such as pyracantha or ceanothus. The 2-4.5 cm long leaves are narrowly elliptic to lanceolate and borne alternately. From the axils of the upper ones dangle solitary, narrow, 2-3.5 cm long greenish-yellow bells that often take on hints of purple as they age. Short ovoid to spherical-shaped 2 cm long berries follow. These vary from plant to plant ripening to deep blue, shades of purple, red or white. The blue form seems to be the commonest in British gardens. In Tasmania it is a common plant and there known as climbing blueberry.

B. scandens (Zone 8-9) (SE Australia, Tasmania) has the same appeal as the previous species but lacks the colourful fruits. It is not unlike *B. longifolia*, but has longer, wavy-edged leaves and flowers with more widely flared petal tips. Pale yellow is the usual colour, but in Tasmania violet and purple forms occur. The 2-3 cm downy fruits are usually olive green, occasionally red.

Bomarea *Alstroemeriaceae*

Between 120 and 150 species are recognised in this genus or at least that number of names are listed, not always the same thing. Many of the species are variable and lots of problems await the attention

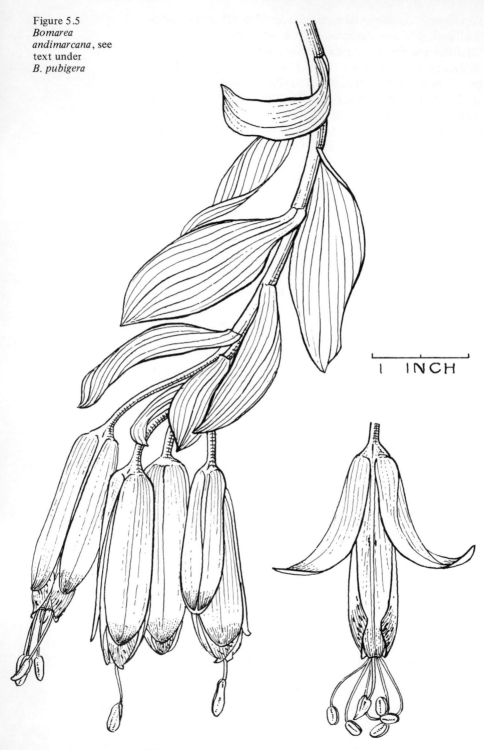

Figure 5.5
*Bomarea
andimarcana*, see
text under
B. pubigera

I INCH

of a bold taxonomic botanist. They are closely related to *Alstroemeria* (Peruvian lily) and have the same narrow upsidedown or on-edge leaves. The flowers, however, are regularly tubular or funnel-shaped, not lopsided as in the Peruvian lily. The genus is spread over S America, up through Central America to Mexico and out to Cuba. Most of the species are twining climbers, but some are prostrate; others lean or scramble in or over shrubs. All are tuberous-rooted, some evergreen, others herbaceous. All but a very few need greenhouse culture in zones less than 9. Ordinary soil is suitable and a sunny, or lightly shaded site. Propagation is by seeds under glass in spring, or division while dormant or after flowering. They make undemanding pot plants and lend an exotic touch to the cool greenhouse.

B. caldasii (Zone 8-9) (Andes, Ecuador to Colombia) twines up to 3 or 4 m, sometimes more, and is perhaps the most handsome of the half-hardy species. The flowers are 4-5 cm long and vary from yellow with a slight touch of red to wholly orange or red, the inner three tepals often spotted brown, red or greenish. Small, thin stems may bear as few as five flowers; strong, robust ones can terminate in huge radiating clusters of 40 or more, a really spectacular sight. On a warm wall it marries well with climbing roses, especially those with cream or white flowers, e.g. 'Alberic Barbier'. In the mild climate of Madeira it is rapidly naturalising itself and looks all set to becoming a member of the extensive cohort of semi-wild plants that form such a prominent part of the flora.

B. edulis (Zone 8) ranges more widely than most species, from Peru to Mexico and Cuba, and varies accordingly. Generally, the flowers on cultivated plants are basically pink to light red on the outside, yellowish or greenish within with red flecks, 2.5-3.5 cm long in clusters of 10-30. It is a twining species, reaching 3 m or more in height, deciduous and surprisingly hardy. A form of this species collected in Peru by Martyn Cheese and John Watson (CW 5268), former colleagues on our expedition to the Chilean Andes in 1971-2, has survived two fairly severe winters at the foot of a south wall in my N Norfolk garden.

B. kalbreyeri (Zone 8-9) (Colombia) has been much confused with *B. caldasii*, at least in recent times in Britain. It generally has smaller flowers, 2.5-3 cm long, with brick-red outer tepals and longer orange-yellow, red-spotted inner ones.

B. pubigera (Zone 9) (CW 5270) was collected in Peru in 1972 (see note under *B. edulis* above) and named at Kew. From a gardener's point of view it appears to be virtually identical with *B. andimarcana*. Both are non-climbing, spearing through or leaning on shrubs for support. Both are evergreen with semi-rigid, erect leafy stems 2-3 m tall which arch over at the top. The leaves are narrowly lance-shaped,

5-12 cm long, with several neatly parallel veins beneath, upon which are borne short, kinky white hairs. From late spring to late autumn and as each new stem reaches full length, clusters of pendent flowers expand. Each one is tubular, 4-5 cm long, minutely white-downy, pale yellow suffused palest red and tipped soft green. Not a showy or beautiful flower, but intriguing and worthy of close appraisal.

Bougainvillea *Nyctaginaceae*

Although 18 species are known in this S American genus of shrubs and climbers, only three and their hybrids are well known. These are flamboyant scramblers familiar to all who travel in the warmer countries. Such is their appeal that, like other very popular plants, e.g. *Antirrhinum*, *Delphinium*, *Dahlia*, the Latin name has become the accepted vernacular one. In this case it is rather nice that Louis Antoine de Bougainville (1729-1811) should be so remembered and honoured, for he was a very distinguished Frenchman indeed, soldier, sailor, scientist, lawyer, navigator and explorer who sailed around the world in 1767-9. As in the equally popular poinsettia, what appear to be the flowers of Bougainvillea are in fact, coloured leaves (bracts), groups of three sheltering three small, narrowly tubular, true flowers. In turn, the trios of bracts and flowers are arranged in large clusters generally carried in abundance. All fertile, humus-rich soils are acceptable, and a site in full sun. In all zones lower than 9, greenhouse conditions are necessary, with a winter minimum of 7°-10°C. Plants in tubs and floor level beds give the best display but much smaller pot plants can be created. For this method of growing, rooted cuttings are potted into 15 cm containers and tied to a 90-120 cm cane. When the plant reaches the top of its cane the tip is pinched out. All lateral stems that grow out below are in turn pinched back when 10-15 cm long. From late autumn to spring the plants are kept dry. About mid-spring, or earlier if desired, the lateral stems are cut back to 2-3 cm long spurs, the root balls are thoroughly watered and the minimum temperature raised to 15°C. Growth is then rapid and a good display of blossom should result. Propagation is by semi-hardwood cuttings, preferably with a heel, in summer. Hardwood cuttings of spring prunings can also be tried with bottom heat of about 21°C.

   B. X *buttiana* (Zone 9) (*B. glabra* X *peruviana*) was originally found as a natural hybrid in a garden in Colombia by Mrs R.V. Butt in 1910. It is much like *B. peruviana*, but taller and with larger leaves and more bunchy flower clusters. The original plant was called 'Mrs Butt' and also acquired the synonym 'Crimson Lake'. It bears a profusion of crimson to magenta bracts and is still one of the most widely grown cultivars. Newer sorts include 'Brilliant', with bracts that start coppery-orange and mature cerise; 'Killie Campbell',

'Orange King' and 'Golden Glow' in varying shades of orange; 'Easter Parade', pink; 'Jamaica White', pure white; 'Mrs MacLean', a dark red sport of 'Mrs Butt'; 'Scarlett O'Hara', brilliant orange-scarlet and crimson; and 'Surprise', a curious but startling chimera with large clusters of bracts which can be all white or all rose-purple or a mixture of the two. Some of these cultivars probably also have *spectabilis* in their parentage. *B. glabra* (Brazil) grows to 4 m or more, is weakly spiny and has elliptic leaves growing to about 8 cm long. The floral bracts are about 4 cm or a little longer, in shades of cyclamen-purple. *B. g.* 'Cypheri' is more robust, with larger leaves and bracts; 'Magnifica' (*B. magnifica* 'Traillii') is similar, but bracts are deep reddish-purple and are produced over a longer period. 'Sanderiana' is like the species in size but extremely floriferous especially when small, and one of the best for pot culture. 'Snow White' has green veined, white bracts. 'Variegata' has the leaves boldly white-variegated and makes a splendid foliage plant; it does not flower prolifically.

B. peruviana (Zone 9) (Colombia to Peru) has stout spines and broadly ovate to rounded leaves. The bracts are rose to magenta-pink. It is seldom grown in Britain, and abroad in warmer countries is rarely grown under its species name, often parading as 'Ecuadorean Pink', 'Lady Hudson' or 'Princess Margaret Rose'.

B. spectabilis (Zone 9) (Brazil) also may have stout spines but is variable in this respect, with ovate leaves, velvety-hairy beneath and sometimes above. The floral bracts vary from pink to light brick-red and purple. Several cultivars are known but seldom seen in cool, temperate zone greenhouses. *B. s. lateritia* is seen occasionally and has long been grown in Tenerife, being clearly distinguished by its poppy-red bracts. 'Carnarvon', which arose in W Australia, is larger and more richly hued.

Boussingaultia, see *Anredera*.

Bowiea Zulu potato *Liliaceae*

Only one of the two African species that form this genus is regularly cultivated. *B. volubilis* (Zone 8-9) is an oddity among the climbers, being a succulent, bulbous plant with a climbing stem and no basal leaves. It grows in dry, scrubby areas in the wilds of S Africa, the large, rounded, greenish bulbs — up to 20 cm wide — sitting at ground level. In the rainy season, slender, fleshy, bright green stems rapidly twine upwards to 2-3 m, then produce many small branches which look like and act as leaves. Finally, six-tepalled, greenish-white, starry flowers about 8 mm wide appear. It needs a rich, sharply drained soil and to be kept more or less dry from autumn to spring. In zones 7 downwards, it needs a frost-free greenhouse. In zone 8 it can be grown at the base of a sheltered, sunny wall if protected from frost and rain with a mound of gravel and a cloche. Propagation is by seeds in spring or by separating the bulbs when they divide naturally.

Brodiaea, see *Dichelostemma*.

C

Calonyction, see *Ipomoea*.

Calystegia (bindweed) *Convolvulaceae*

Although often beautiful, most of the 25 species here are invasive plants and some are notorious, near-ineradicable weeds. They are perennials with deeply delving, slender rhizomes and vigorous, twining stems. Their flowers are funnel-shaped, distinguished from the closely allied *Convolvulus* by the presence of two large bracteoles which enclose the calyx. All ordinary soils are acceptable, and a site in the sun or partial shade. Propagation is by division during the dormant season or seeds in spring.

C. hederacea (*C. japonica*) (E Asia) climbs to 5 m or more, with narrow arrow-shaped leaves growing to 6 cm long and pink flowers about 4-5 cm long. It is almost exclusively represented in gardens by *C. h.* 'Flore Pleno' ('Plena', *C. pubescens*) with a fully double sterile flower known in the USA as California rose. In areas with rich soils and warm summers, this can be invasive and in parts of the USA it has long been naturalised. In Britain and other areas with similar cool or uncertain summers it is not invasive and usually needs a sheltered site to thrive.

C. sepium (Zone 5-6) (hedge bindweed) and *C. sylvatica* (large bindweed), both widespread in temperate regions, are mentioned purely as a warning. Both are extremely decorative, especially the pink subspecies *pulchra*, but their nuisance value as weeds soon surpasses their beauty.

Campsis (trumpet vine) *Bignoniaceae*

Both of the species that form this genus are showy, choice, deciduous self-clingers. They have opposite pairs of ash-like pinnate leaves and terminal trusses of funnel-shaped flowers with five spreading, rounded petals in late summer. They grow in a wide variety of fertile soils, but in zones 4-8 need a sheltered site. In areas with cool summers, e.g. Britain, a sunny site is essential to ripen the wood and ensure a crop of flowers. Propagation is easiest by layering or removing rooted suckers in spring. Semi-hardwood cuttings can be taken in late summer and some success can usually be had with hardwood cuttings in autumn. Root cuttings can be tried in spring under glass.

C. grandiflora (Zone 7) (China) has the largest flowers, 6 cm or more long by 7.5-9 cm across the lobes. The throat of each flower is orange with red veins, the lobes paler, ranging from apricot-pink to peach, and darkest when newly open. Capable of climbing 6-10 m it is a root climber but not very secure and in cool summer areas often needs to be tied at least partially to its support. It has a wide range in its native land, from the north where winters are cold right down to the tropical climate of Hainan.

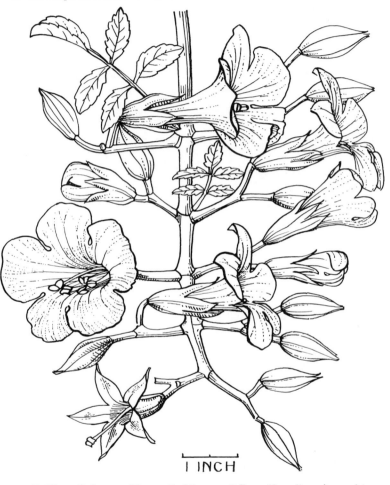

Figure 5.6
Campsis grandiflora

I INCH

C. X *tagliabuana* (Zone 4) (*C. grandiflora* X *radicans*) combines the best characters of both parents particularly in the cultivar called 'Mme Galen', a French selection raised prior to 1889 when it began its nursery life. It has salmon-red flowers, more freely borne than those of its Chinese parent (at least in Britain) and clings to its support rather more securely.

C. radicans (Zone 4) (South-eastern USA) looks splendid climbing up trees 8-12 m tall, as it does in its native country. In those areas where it is abundant it is a great opportunist, climbing up telephone poles and walls and sometimes making a nuisance of itself. Unlike *C. grandiflora*, it is an efficient root climber and seldom needs aid to hang on once established. When well flowered it presents a flamboyant sight with its orange-tubed, scarlet-petalled flowers. It is, however, a rather untidy grower and never gives the display in Britain that it does in countries with warmer summers.

Figure 5.7
Campsis grandiflora
seed pods

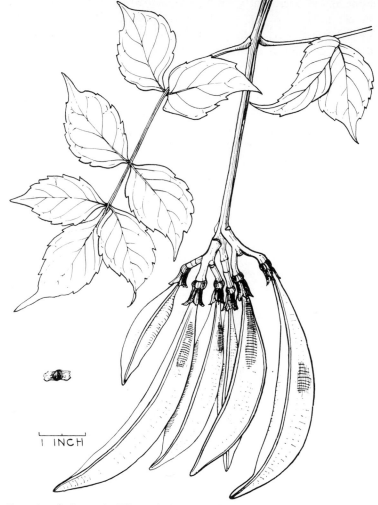

1 INCH

Canarina (African bellflower) *Campanulaceae*

This genus of three species is very closely allied to the bellflowers (*Campanula*), but differs in that its leaves are carried in opposite pairs, or whorls of three, and it has edible berry fruits. They are true scramblers, sending up strong stems through bushes and low trees and there becoming anchored by pairs or whorls of horizontal branches. They come from areas with long dry summers and mild to warm, moist winters. The rootstock is a rather woody tuber which starts into growth when the rains come in autumn. Flowering takes place from late autumn to spring and the plant dies away by mid-summer. In all zones less than 9 it needs greenhouse treatment with a winter minimum of 10°C, though short spells down to 7°C will do no harm. The tubers should be repotted annually in late summer, using any standard potting mix. When growth commences the plant should be kept regularly watered, then dried off again about six weeks after flowering. Propagation is by cuttings of young shoots in autumn, or seeds in late spring or summer.

C. canariensis (Zone 9) (Canary Islands bellflower) is endemic to the Canary Islands and the only species in general cultivation. It grows 2-3 m tall with narrowly triangular, irregularly-toothed leaves 5-8 cm long. When almost full grown, the strongest stem tips terminate in pendent, elegantly formed, waxy orange bells to 6 cm long. The berries which follow are ovoid, reddish to black. Although less common than formerly, it can still be seen in the Canary Islands and makes a fine excuse to visit that favoured place. I still treasure memories of seeing it, very unexpectedly, on a steep, rocky slope scrambling through naturalised brambles. (It is mainly found in the evergreen forest).

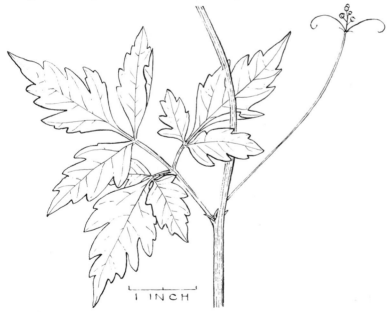

Figure 5.8
A single leaf and flower cluster of *Cardiospermum*. The two tendrils are derived from flower buds

1 INCH

Cardiospermum (heart seed) *Sapindaceae*

Only one member of this twelve species genus from the tropics and sub-tropics is in general cultivation. This is *C. halicacabum*, (Zone 5 as an annual, Zone 9 as perennial) also known as heart pea and balloon vine. It is a woody stemmed, tropical American plant but often grown as a half-hardy annual in Britain and other cold winter areas. It provides an interesting example of flowers modified as tendrils. The axillary racemes of flowers are long-stalked, the first two buds being reduced to or replaced by tendrils. The leaves are divided into nine, lobed and slender pointed leaflets, usually of a pale to bright green. The tiny, four-petalled white flowers are followed by balloon-like, membranous seed capsules 2-3 cm wide, containing black seeds, each bearing a white, heart-shaped mark at its point of attachment. In one season a well grown plant can exceed 3 m in height. In the tropics it grows very much taller. Any moisture retentive, but well-drained, soil is suitable and a site in sun sheltered from strong winds. Propagation is by seeds under glass in spring at 18°C, ideally sown singly in 7.5 cm containers.

Celastrus *Celastraceae*

Approximately 30 species of shrubs and twining climbers form this mainly tropical and sub-tropical genus. Several of the hardier, deciduous kinds are cultivated for their coloured fruits and autumn foliage. They have elliptic to ovate, alternate leaves, small five-petalled greenish to yellowish flowers in groups in the leaf axils, and rounded fruits. The latter split open when ripe to show several seeds, each covered with a bright, usually red, fleshy coat called an aril. They grow well in ordinary soil and in sun or partial shade. Propagation is by seeds when ripe or layering, and removing rooted suckers in early spring.

C. articulatus, see *C. orbiculatus*.

C. hypoleucus (Zone 7) (*C. hypoglaucus*) (China) can climb up to 6 m or more and makes a fine plant for a tree. It has oblong to obovate leaves 10-15 cm long and young shoots surfaced with a purplish, waxy patina. Unlike most other hardy species it has quite long racemes of yellowish flowers. In fruit, each raceme can elongate up to 20 cm with fruits the size of a large pea. The inner surface of the fruit is yellow, the seed arils red. It was introduced by E.H. Wilson about 1900 having previously been discovered by Augustine Henry.

C. orbiculatus (Zone 4) (*C. articulatus*) is the best-known species. It is found throughout north eastern Asia but did not reach Britain until 1870 — via America and Professor Charles Sprague Sargent, first Director of the Arnold Arboretum. Later, seed came direct from China. *Orbiculatus* refers to the rounded, 5 cm long leaves, though some are rather more obovate in outline. They turn yellow in autumn. Tiny, yellowish-green flowers appear in late spring and are followed by pea-sized fruits. These open to disclose scarlet seeds backgrounded against the glossy, yellow capsule valves. They come into their own when the leaves fall. When a good crop of fruit wreathes all the supple stems, this is one of the finest climbers for winter effect, the low rays of the sun at that time of the year illuminating the yellow and red to perfection. It is not a favourite of the birds. *C. orbiculatus* is, however, dioecious, and it is important to obtain a hermaphrodite form or fruits will not appear.

C. rosthornianus (Zone 6) (China) is rather of the style of *C. orbiculatus*, but with narrower, glossier leaves set on very slender stems which often loop down in pendent fashion.

C. rugosus (Zone 6) (China) was discovered and introduced by E.H. Wilson in 1904. It is another species allied to *C. orbiculatus* but rendered most distinctive by its warted stems and finely wrinkled leaves, boldly veined beneath.

C. scandens (Zone 2) is N America's answer to *C. orbiculatus* and in its homeland is an equally fine plant, though even there, not as free-fruiting as it might be. In Britain it is decidedly shy in this respect. Furthermore it is dioecious and no hermaphrodite plants are known. It has mainly ovate leaves and larger than pea-sized fruits which are orange within and contain scarlet seeds. In Australia and New Zealand it is confused with *C. orbiculatus*.

Ceropegia (fountain flower) *Asclepiadaceae*

About 160 shrubby and twining perennials, some tuberous rooted, comprise this genus. They are natives of tropical and sub-tropical Asia and Africa, including Malagasy and the Canary Islands, often dry, semi-desert regions. The unique flowers parallel those of *Aristolochia* (q.v.), but the tubular portion is more obvious and the expanded mouth perfectly regular with distinct petal-lobes which stay joined at their tips and create a cage-like structure. In all zones lower than 9 they are greenhouse plants, making interesting pot plants. A sharply-drained rooting medium is essential, e.g. a standard mix with extra coarse sand or grit added. Sun and a minimum temperature of 10°C are necessary for healthy growth. All the species mentioned here should be kept almost dry from late autumn to mid-spring. Propagation is by seeds in spring or cuttings in summer at not less than 18°C.

C. caffrorum (Zone 9-10) (lamp flower) (*C. linearis*) (SE Africa) grows to 1 m or more, the wiry stems bearing pairs of lanceolate, dark green leaves to 3 cm long. The flowers are in clusters of three to five, each one 2-3 cm long, green with purple stripes and finely hairy.

C. haygarthii (Zone 9-10) (S Africa) is considered by some to be the most beautiful. It certainly has a fascinating flower, 5-7 cm long with a cream to pale pink, maroon-spotted tube bent sharply at the base and flaring widely at the mouth. The five narrow lobes stretch star-like across the top and from the centre arises a maroon, stigma-

Figure 5.9
*Ceropegia
sandersonii*

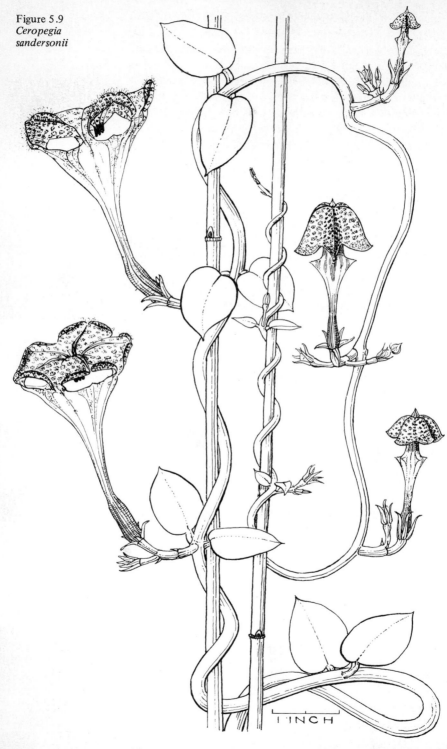

Rosa 'Mme Gregoire Stachelin' and *Lonicera x americana*

Rosa 'Mme Gregoire Stachelin'

Streptosolen jamesonii

Actinidia kolomitka

Clematis montana rubens

Lonicera x americana

Hedera helix 'Buttercup'

Canarina canariensis

Rosa 'Frances Lester'

Tropaeolum speciosum

like organ bearing a red, hairy, hollow knob about 8 mm wide, like a bizarre topknot. The plant twines up to 1 m with fairly robust stems and ovate-cordate leaves 2-5 cm long.

C. sandersonii (Zone 9-10) (parachute plant, fountain flower) (Natal) is akin to *C. haygarthii* and much like it in habit and foliage. The flower, however, is highly distinctive. Each one is about 7 cm long, pale green lined and mottled darker. The tube is straight, then expands abruptly at the mouth to a wide funnel with five little peg-like petal lobes. Across these lobes is spread a parasol-like membrane complete with fringe. The likeness — in a fanciful way — to both a parachute and a stylised fountain is remarkable.

Cissus (Kangaroo vine) *Vitidaceae*

This varied genus of 350 more or less tropical species contains tendril climbers (some succulent) and succulent shrubs. The things they have in common are alternate, simple or compound leaves, tiny, usually greenish, four-petalled flowers and berry-like, barely fleshy to dry fruits. All respond well to pot or tub culture and one of the standard potting mixes. *C. cactiformis* must be kept on the dry side in winter. Propagation is by seeds in spring or cuttings in summer.

C. antarctica (Zone 9-10) (Kangaroo vine) comes from eastern Australia, ranging through Queensland and New South Wales. It can attain 5 m or more in height given the opportunity, and in zones 9 and 10 makes an effective screening plant. Elsewhere it needs a winter minimum of 7°-10°C, and has become a popular and tolerant house plant. The foliage is dense, each leaf being 7-15 cm long, ovate, boldly toothed and a lustrous rich green colour.

C. cactiformis (Zone 9-10) (E Africa) provides a good example of a succulent climber. It grows to 3 m high, with sparingly branched stems 2-5 cm thick and constricted at the nodes. They are fleshy but firm, quadrangular in cross section, the angles with horny, serrated edges. The small, ovate leaves appear on young stems only and soon fall. *C. quadrangularis* is cast in a similar mould, but the stem sections are slimmer and less fleshy, the angles more or less winged. They have a bluish-grey patina particularly when young.

C. discolor (Zone 10) (rex begonia vine) (Cambodia, Java) can only be grown outside in zone 10, but makes a splendid foliage pot plant for the home or greenhouse with a minimum temperature of 15°-18°C. It has oblong-ovate, cordate-based leaves 10-15 cm long, somewhat quilted above and deep velvety-green with silvery-white bands between the veins. The lower surfaces are maroon.

C. rhombifolia (Zone 9-10) (Mexico to Brazil and W Indies) is much confused, at least in Britain, with *Rhoicissus rhomboidea*. Both are popular houseplants with trifoliate, coarsely toothed, dark green, lustrous leaves. The easy identification feature is the forked tendrils. (Those of the rhoicissus are unbranched).

C. sicyoides (Zone 9-10) (tropical America, S Florida) is sometimes known as princess vine and is used as a house plant. In zone 10 and the warmer parts of 9, it is a fine foliage plant, useful as a screen or covering a shady arbour. Where humidity is high, long, aerial roots hang like a curtain. The leaves are heart-shaped, about 10 cm in length and of a pleasing light green.

C. striata (Zone 8-9) (Brazil to Chile) has formerly been known as *Vitis striata* and *Ampelopsis sempervirens*. It is the hardiest of the species, surviving in sheltered parts of zone 8 unless the winter is exceptionally severe. Of elegant growth and capable of attaining 10 m or more in height, it has slender, zig-zag stems set with sucker-tipped tendrils and neat, dark green leaves. The latter are composed of three to five oblanceolate, lightly toothed leaflets. The tiny flowers give way to pea-sized, polished black berries. This plant is widespread in its native land and has been called the 'ivy of Uruguay', presumably because of its ubiquity in that country. I did not see very much of it when collecting in Chile, but in one small area of woodland it behaved like a jungle liane, very effectively lacing the branches together. Although comparatively slender, one of its looped stems was strong enough to support my eleven and a half-stone weight when swung upon!

Clematis *Ranunculaceae*

Among the 250 species credited to this genus are some of the best known and most popular of all hardy climbers. The genus has a cosmopolitan distribution, but mainly from temperate climates. Not all its members are climbers. Those that are, have compound leaves, the long stalks of the leaflets acting as tendrils. The flowers may be solitary or in panicles, composed of four to six, sometimes more, petaloid sepals. The latter may open out flat, point down to form a bell or appear to be moulded tightly together to form an urn, e.g. *C. texensis*. Several species have attractive seed heads formed as a cluster of tiny nutlets known as achenes, each one surmounted by a slender, feathery awn. In general they luxuriate in humus-rich, moisture retentive but well-drained soil, ideally with the root area in shade and the tops in sun. Propagation is by layering in spring or stem and leaf bud cuttings during the later part of summer. Species clematis do not need pruning, except to curb over-exuberant top growth and thin out congested stems. Cultivars derived from *C. viticella* and *C.* X *jackmannii* are best cut back to the lowest pair of buds on each previous year's stem or, if several stems arise from below the soil, to ground level. This must be done in late winter just as the buds start to swell and before they elongate, which they do very early and rapidly in spring. Pruning of the other hybrid groups is optional; leave unless the allotted space is restricted.

C. aethusifolia (Zone 4) (N China) deserves wider recognition, being ideal for the small garden or restricted area. It is almost a miniature, rarely reaching above 2 m in height, with ferny, pinnate to bipinnate leaves composed of tiny, deeply-lobed leaflets. The pale yellow, nodding flowers are bell-shaped, to 2 cm long, and open from late summer to autumn and are followed by decorative, plumy white seed heads.

C. afoliata (Zone 8-9) (New Zealand) is perhaps the most unusual and atypical of all the climbing clematis species. Young plants have small, trifoliate leaves, but adult ones are vitually leafless, only the midribs remaining as tendrils. Smooth yellowish green, rush-like stems climb to 3 m and in late spring bear dioecious, bell-shaped, pale green, yellow tinted, fragrant flowers in axillary clusters. Scrambling up a large wall shrub such as pyracantha, it makes an interesting talking point. It will not stand prolonged winter cold.

C. alpina (Zone 5) (*Atragene alpina*) has a wide range in N Europe and N Asia and in the mountains farther south. It has stems 2-3 m long clad with 7-15 cm long leaves, each one composed of six to nine boldly toothed, ovate leaflets. In late spring, elegantly nodding blue flowers appear singly in the leaf axils. There are four, pointed sepals disposed to form a wide bell centred with tiny, spoon-shaped white petals or staminodes, and yellow stamens. The seed heads are silvery-grey. The colouring of the flowers varies in intensity among seed-raised plants. 'Frances Rivis' ('Blue Giant') has the largest and bluest blooms; 'Columbine' is almost as big and pale blue; 'Ruby' is red. *C. a. sibirica* has cream flowers and occurs wild in Siberia to NE Europe; 'White Moth' is a pure white selection.

C. armandii (Zone 7) (China) is undoubtedly the best of the few evergreen clematis species and in my view ranks among the top ten in the genus as a whole. Fast growing to 10 m or more, it has trifoliate leaves, the leaflets leathery, smooth-edged and lustrous, the longest to 15 cm. When young they are flushed coppery-red. Variably composed of four to seven sepals, the wide open white flowers appear in axillary clusters in spring, often in profusion. The overall effect is of a superior evergreen *C. montana*, and its lack of complete winter hardiness is to be regretted. Seed-raised plants can have inferior flowers and the named clone 'Snowdrift' should be obtained. 'Apple Blossom' is a delightful pink cultivar.

C. balearica, see *C. cirrhosa*.

C. X 'Beauty of Worcester' (Zone 6) (large-flowered hybrid) bears both single and double flowers, a feat in itself, though the single are nicer; violet-blue with contrasting, creamy-white stamens. They open from early summer to autumn.

C. X 'Belle of Woking' (Zone 6) (large-flowered hybrid) usually has simple broad leaves and, in early summer, sumptuous, fully double mauve flowers with a silvery lustre. On a vigorous plant they can be 15 cm wide.

C. campaniflora (Zone 6) (Portugal, S Spain) has an obvious affinity to *C. viticella*, with the same growth habit but more highly dissected leaves. It climbs to 5 m or more and from late summer to autumn can become covered with white, blue-tinted, bowl-shaped, nodding flowers with engagingly upturned sepal tips.

C. chrysocoma (Zone 7) (China) can be described as a less vigorous, less hardy but more beautiful version of the familiar *C. montana*. Further distinctions are the yellowish hairs on young stems and flower stalks and the remontant flowering habit. The flowers too are always white, tinged pink. This description refers to plants in cultivation. According to *Trees and Shrubs Hardy in the British Isles* by W.J. Bean, eighth edition, vol. 1, p. 640, this plant is a shrub to 2.5 m, with *C. c. sericea* (*C. spooneri*) as a climbing variety. There would appear to be some abiguity or confusion that needs clarifying.

C. cirrhosa (Zone 7) (S Europe to western Turkey) climbs to 3 m or so given the chance, but its very slender growth seems happiest rambling through lower shrubs. It is unique among the more commonly cultivated clematis in blooming in winter and spring and, though of modest beauty, is invaluable for this reason. The flowers are bell-shaped, pendent, creamy-white and borne in axillary pairs or singly. They are followed by almost white, fluffy seed heads. Both flowers and fruit are nicely backed by elegantly dissected evergreen leaves of almost fern-like delicacy. *C. c. balearica* is restricted to the Balearic Islands and has even more elegant foliage plus flowers that are spotted red-purple within. It thrives near the sea, a fact that will not surprise early holiday makers to Majorca where it is not infrequent rambling through scrub overlooking the Mediterranean. Despite its homeland, it is surprisingly hardy, surviving in my N Norfolk garden when the temperature dropped to $-18°C$ one night in January 1979.

C. X 'Comtesse de Bouchard' (Zone 6) (large-flowered hybrid) is a vigorous cultivar and very free with its lively pink, mauve-shaded flowers that open in summer. It received the RHS Award of Merit in 1936 and the Award of Garden Merit in 1969.

C. crispa (Zone 5) (south eastern USA) belongs to the *Viorna* group of clematis, the best known member in cultivation being *C. texensis*. It is sub-shrubby, most of the top growth dying back in winter. In a warm summer the stems can exceed 2 m but are often less. The leaves are basically pinnate, but the leaflets may in turn be divided in trifoliate fashion or lobed in various ways. From mid to late summer, 4-5 cm long nodding flowers appear on slender, solitary, axillary stalks. Each flower is 3-5 cm long, bell-shaped, fragrant; the four leathery sepals are blue-purple with pale to whitish edges. In its homeland, this species inhabits swampy and low lying woods and in cultivation stands wetter soil conditions than most other clematis.

C. X *durandii* (Zone 5) combines the genes of the herbaceous perennial, *C. integrifolia* and the climbing *C.* X *jackmannii* to great effect. Achieving up to 3 m in height, it has simple ovate leaves and deep violet-blue flowers up to 10 cm or so in width, from mid-summer to autumn. The seed heads are attractive.

C. X *eriostemon* (Zone 5) is, like the previous plant, a hybrid involving the herbaceous perennial *C. integrifolia*, in this case with *C. viticella* as the other parent. It favours the former parent and is only marginally a climber, its 1.5-2.5 m tall stems needing the support of well branched twiggy sticks. The purple-blue flowers are nodding on slender stalks and have sepals with recurved tips. They are backed by dark leaves which range from single to pinnately dissected. This description refers to the cultivar 'Hendersonii' which represents it in cultivation.

C. X 'Ernest Markham' (Zone 6) (large-flowered hybrid) bears glorious petunia-red flowers 10-15 cm wide with a contrasting boss of yellow stamens. If lightly pruned, flowering starts around mid-summer. If hard pruned, the display begins later but goes on into autumn.

C. X 'Etoile Violette' (Zone 6) (large-flowered hybrid) undoubtedly has *C. viticella* somewhere in its ancestry, though the flowers open out flat — to about 10 cm and are mostly six-sepalled. They are a satisfying shade of rich purple with cream stamens and are borne in elegant fashion.

C. fargesii (Zone 5) (China) deserves to be better known, with its light, matt green compound leaves and succession of 5-6 cm wide pure white flowers. The latter open out flat and are composed of six sepals. The first ones open about mid-summer, the last fade in late autumn. It is usually represented in cultivation by *C. f. souliei*, a variant separated by minute botanical characters.

C. finetiana (Zone 7) (China) is in effect, a less hardy, smaller-flowered, less vigorous version of *C. armandii* which blooms four to six weeks later.

C. flammula (Zone 6) (S Europe) climbs vigorously to 5 m and forms glorious tangles of wiry stems, which in late summer and autumn terminate in 30 cm long panicles of small, fragrant white flowers. The leaves are formed of three to five bright green leaflets which may be lanceolate or almost orbicular and lobed or cleft.

C. florida (Zone 6) (China) was first seen by a western botanist, Carl Peter Thunberg (1743-1828), in Japan where it had long been cultivated. Thunberg introduced it in 1776. Later, Augustine Henry found the original wild species in the wilds of Hupeh, and later

71

E.H. Wilson introduced it into Britain. It is a deciduous to semi-evergreen climber rarely above 2.5-3.5 m high, with leaves composed of six to nine leaflets. The widely expanded flowers are 6-8 cm wide, formed of four to six white to cream, oval sepals, the back of each one bearing a longitudinal greenish band. Deep purple stamens provide a charming contrast. They open in mid to late summer. Best known in gardens is *C. f.* 'Sieboldii' ('Bicolor') with flowers of the larger size and invariably with six petals plus a sizeable boss of purple petaloid stamens. In the now very rare — or possibly extinct — cultivar 'Plena', the petaloids are white. Some botanical authorities unite *C. patens* with this species and the two are obviously very closely akin.

C. forrestii, see *C. napaulensis.*

C. fusca (Zone 4) (NE Asia) is a semi-herbaceous climber to about 3m tall and after the style of *C. viticella*. But there the image ends, for the 2-3 cm long purplish to brownish-red urn-shaped flowers hang solitarily close to the leaf axil and need to be looked for. It is not without a modest charm, however, and always intrigues the novice clematophile.

C. X 'Gipsy Queen' (Zone 6) (large-flowered hybrid) grows vigorously and from mid-summer to early autumn bears 13 cm wide velvety purple flowers which take on reddish tones as they age.

C. glauca (Zone 5) (W China and adjacent Siberia) can be likened to its near ally *C. orientalis* but produces wider open, deep orange-yellow flowers.

C. grata (Zone 6) (Himalayas to China) is represented in cultivation by the Chinese variety *C. g. grandidentata*, a vigorous climber growing to 10 m in height. It has grey downy compound leaves to 15 cm long and small terminal and axillary panicles of 2.5 cm wide white flowers in early summer. It is akin to the familiar European old-man's-beard (*C. vitalba*), but much more effective in bloom and with similar seed heads. See also *C.* X *jouiniana.*

C. graveolens, see *C. orientalis.*

C. X 'Hagley Hybrid' (Zone 6) (large-flowered hybrid) is ideal for a restricted site, rarely exceeding 2.5 m and producing its 13 cm wide pink flowers in abundance from mid-summer to autumn.

C. X 'Henryi' (Zone 6) ('Henryana', 'Bangholme Belle') (large-flowered hybrid) is a primary hybrid of quality, being directly derived from *C. lanuginosa*. Its shapely 15-18 cm wide flowers are elegantly poised like huge white butterflies. The best display comes in early summer with an encore in the autumn. It received the RHS Award of Garden Merit in 1973.

C. hookerana (Zone 8-9) (*C. colensoi*) is one of the charming evergreen New Zealand species, somewhat reminiscent in growth of *C. cirrhosa balearica*, but with starry, five-sepalled, silky, green-tinted yellow flowers to 4 cm wide. The flowers appear in early summer and are sweetly fragrant. It looks very appealing rambling over a shrub, but needs a cool greenhouse in zones lower than 8.

C. indivisa, see *C. paniculata*.

C. X *jackmanii* (Zone 5) is without doubt the most famous of all the primary clematis hybrids. It arose at the nursery of George Jackman, Woking, Surrey, in 1860 as a result of crossing *C. lanuginosa* with *C. viticella*. Reaching 3 m or more in height, it resembles a coarser-leaved, more robust *viticella* with wider flowers 10-13 cm across and of a rich and glorious shade of velvety-purple. The best-known cultivar, 'Superba', has similar flowers but with a strong hint of maroon-red. With other Asiatic species, notably *florida*, *patens* and *lanuginosa*, this hybrid has played a part in the development of the large-flowered cultivar group.

C. X *jouiniana* (Zone 4) sometimes masquerades as the true *C. grata*, though the two are easily separated. *Jouiniana* is a hybrid between the old-man's-beard, *C. vitalba*, and the herbaceous woody-based perennial *C. heracleifolia*. A climber to 3 m or so and needing plenty of support, it can also be used as a passable and unusual ground cover. The leaves have three to five broadly lobed and toothed leaflets up to about 10 cm long. They are a rich, semi-matt green above and paler and almost glossy beneath, quite unlike the grey downy surfaces of *C. grata*. The flowers are small, formed of four narrow and pointed sepals about 2 cm long, but borne in sizeable terminal panicles in late summer and autumn. In the usual form the flowers are yellow-white to cream, suffused bluish-lilac — a much nicer blend than it sounds, especially *en masse*.

C. X 'Lady Betty Balfour' (Zone 6) (large-flowered hybrid) has both vigour and beauty, with coppery-tinted young leaves and 13-15 cm wide six-sepalled flowers of violet-blue ageing to a paler, bluer shade. It needs a sunny site to perform well and blooms in late summer and autumn.

C. lanuginosa (Zone 6) (China) appears to be very rare in cultivation, at least in Britain. It is closely related to the *C. patens-florida* complex but is smaller, being 2-3 m at most. It has simple and trifoliate leaves up to 13 cm long which are softly grey woolly beneath. The flower stalks and buds are similarly woolly, the latter expanding flat to 10-15 cm wide and composed of six to eight white sepals. Although rare and perhaps even extinct in gardens, this species has played a major role in the breeding of the large-flowered hybrids — as typified by the ubiquitous 'Nellie Moser'.

C. lasiandra (Zone 5) (China and Japan), though interesting, can never be described as beautiful. Its main attraction are the triplets of grey-purple, 1-1.5 cm long bell flowers which nod from the upper leaf axils in autumn. The leaves, which are carried on slightly sticky, angled stems, are formed of three to nine-lobed leaflets.

C. X 'Lasurstern' (Zone 6) (large-flowered hybrid) bears 15-20 cm wide flowers of a gloriously rich lavender blue in early summer and again in autumn. It thrives best in sun.

C. macropetala (Zone 5) (China, Siberia) has, like *C. alpina*, been classified in the genus *Atragene*, its flowers possessing the same sort of petaloids or small petals that make that alternative genus possible. It is closely related to *alpina* and much like it in many ways, but is more vigorous, growing to a height of 2.5 m, and with generally smaller leaflets. The violet-blue flowers are larger, 6-8 cm wide, and with larger and more numerous petaloids, some blue, some white. They appear in early summer. *C. m.* 'Markhams Pink' has flowers of lavender-rose, while 'Maidwell Hall' is a truer blue.

C. maximowicziana (Zone 5) (*C. paniculata, C. flammula robusta*) is an extra robust version of *C. flammula* from China, Japan and Korea. In the cool summers of Britain it seldom flowers profusely enough to be worthwhile. Where summers are long and warm it produces its scented white flowers in utmost profligacy and is then a splendid sight.

C. meyeniana (Zone 7-8) (S China, Japan, Taiwan, Philippines) is like *C. finetiana*, another variation on a theme of *armandii*, but with larger, individual clusters of four-sepalled white flowers on a less hardy plant.

C. montana (Zone 5) (Himalayas to China) was introduced to Britain by Lady Sarah Amherst in 1831 and is the most widely planted of all the true species. It is very vigorous, easily reaching 10 m in a tree and then cascading down in a foam of white, four-sepalled flowers. Individual blooms are 5-6 cm wide and appear with bronzy young leaves in late spring and early summer. *C. montana rubens* with pink flowers and purple-bronze young leaves is the most popular form, being even more freely-blooming and reliable. It was introduced from China by E.H. Wilson in 1900. 'Tetrarose' is a tetraploid clone with somewhat larger flowers of a mauve-pink shade raised in Holland. 'Marjorie' is a newcomer with semi-double creamy-pink blooms. *C. m. grandiflora* is also Chinese, but with white flowers to 7.5 cm wide; *C. m. wilsonii* is similar but flowers in late summer.

C. X 'Mrs Cholmondeley' (Zone 6) (large-flowered hybrid) will thrive in any aspect, is vigorous and free-flowering bearing 20 cm wide flowers in abundance in summer and autumn. The pointed sepals are lavender blue with a darker veining, fading gracefully as they age.

C. napaulensis (Zone 8) (*C. forrestii*) is native to SW China and N India and where it is usually evergreen. In Britain it is semi-deciduous and needs a sheltered corner. It has leaves of three to five leaflets on stems to 9 m or so. The 2-3 cm long pale yellow, purplestamened flowers are borne in axillary clusters and, like those of its Mediterranean ally *C. cirrhosa*, open in winter, temperature permitting. In all zones below 9, this species is best in a cool greenhouse. It remains lamentably rare in British gardens despite being introduced by George Forrest as long ago as 1912.

C. X 'Nellie Moser' (Zone 6) (large-flowered hybrid) gained the RHS Award of Garden Merit in 1969. Good though it is, it is grossly over-planted, the more so when there are so many other lovely cultivars to choose from. Its mauve-pink, carmine-striped flowers are variable, often from year to year and on the same plant and in full sun it tends to bleach quickly.

C. X 'Niobe' (Zone 6) (large-flowered hybrid) is a recent cultivar from Poland and received a Gold Medal at the Herfstweelde in Boskoop in 1978. It has deep ruby-red flowers 15 cm or more in width with a boss of yellow stamens, opening from mid-summer to autumn.

C. orientalis (Zone 6) (*C. graveolens*) has a wide range in the wild, from Arabia through the Himalayas to N China. Even without its unusual flowers it would be worth growing for the dissected blue-grey tinted leaves that have an almost fern-like delicacy. Contrasting arrestingly are the yellow lantern flowers each 4-5 cm long and poised nodding on a slender stalk. Late summer and autumn is the period of display and decorative, spherical silky seed heads follow. Several variants are known, the most strikingly attractive being one collected by Ludlow, Sherriff and Elliott in the Himalayas during 1947. This is still usually listed as LSE 13372. It has extra thick, orange-yellow, spongy-textured sepals, a characteristic earning it the name 'orange-peel clematis'.

C. paniculata (Zone 8) (*C. indivisa*, *maximowicziana*) is a New Zealander of charm with trifoliate, evergreen, glossy leaves and 5-10 cm wide unisexual white flowers in airy panicles up to 30 cm long. But for its tenderness it would surely be more popular in Britain where it needs the warmest and most sheltered site. It can be a delightful sight garlanding a large shrub or small tree or climbing up a wall shrub such as pyracantha. *C. p.* 'Lobata' has leaflets which are permanently lobed or boldly toothed, as indeed are those of most young plants when raised from seed, losing them as they mature.

C. patens (Zone 6) (Japan, China) closely resembles *C. florida* and some botanists make it a variety of that species. It is of similar vigour and habit, but the leaves are composed of three to five leaflets (up to nine in *florida*) and the flower stalks lack the two bracts that characterise those of *florida*. The flowers are larger, 10-15 cm wide with usually six to eight sepals. With *florida* and *lanuginosa* it has played an important part in the history of the large-flowered hybrid group.

C. X 'Perle de Azur' (Zone 6) (large-flowered hybrid) is a strong-growing plant to about 4 m and bears a profusion of flowers from mid to late summer. Each bloom is about 15 cm wide and a glorious shade of light blue shading to purplish pink in the centre.

Figure 5.10
Clematis phlebantha

⌐ INCH

C. phlebantha (Zone ?8-9) (Nepal) is the most recently described species, being found in 1952 during the British Museum Expedition to western Nepal and initially distributed under the number PSW 3436. (The Expedition members were O. Polunin, W.R. Sykes and L.H.J. Williams.) Although described as a trailer in the wild it is a climber growing to several metres, particularly in a greenhouse, where it needs to be in zones less than 8. Even in zone 8 it needs the most sheltered site and is often cut back to ground level. Unique among its fellow species, *phlebantha* is completely covered with glistening hairs. The pinnate leaves are particularly attractive, silky above and woolly beneath. The flowers, which appear singly in the upper leaf axils, are up to 5 cm wide and formed of five to seven red-veined white sepals. They open in the latter part of summer.

C. pitcheri (Zone 5) (Central USA) comes into the intriguing, rather than beautiful, category. It climbs 3-4 m and the pinnate leaves are composed of up to seven ovate leaflets, the lowest pair being much bigger than the rest. From late summer into autumn, 2-3 cm long, pendent, tubby, urn-shaped, purplish-blue flowers open in the upper leaf axils. It is a near ally of the better known *C. texensis*, with which it has been hybridised, but it is less herbaceous in character.

C. rehderiana (Zone 6) (*C. nutans*) (China) can reach 10 m and looks splendid garlanding a tree with its ample lobed and toothed light green hairy leaves. In late summer and autumn showers of small, but elegantly formed, primrose bells expand, each one exhaling a fragrance reminiscent of cowslips. Although it received the RHS Award of Merit in 1936 and the Award of Garden Merit in 1969 it is still seen all too seldom. Anyone looking for something different, either among clematis or climbers in general, should give it a try.

C. serratifolia (Zone 5) (Korea) is like a smaller version of *C. tangutica*, producing its lesser bells in greater abundance.

C. songarica (Zone 5) (Turkestan to Siberia) only just qualifies as a climber, its 1.5-2 m stems rambling sideways rather than scaling the heights. It has simple leaves, lance-shaped to linear, smooth and sea-green tinted, which are pleasant in themselves and nicely back the small cream flowers. The latter open in summer and autumn and are followed by plumy seed heads.

C. spooneri, see *C. chrysocoma*.

C. tangutica (Zone 5) (*C. orientalis tangutica*) (Central Asia) is without doubt, the most widely planted species, with lantern-shaped yellow flowers. It is closely related to *C. orientalis* but more vigorous and easily reaching 5-6 m in a tree or up a wall. The sea-green ferny foliage is particularly decorative and the flights of bright yellow 4-5 cm long flowers a constant delight from mid-summer to autumn. It flowers most prolifically in autumn, then adding silvery, silky seed heads to the performance. This fine climber reached Britain (at Kew Gardens) via St Petersburg (now Leningrad) in 1898, but most of the stock now grown here springs from William Purdom, the Lakeland plant collector who found it in Kansu in about 1910. Plants grown from his seed at the RHS Gardens, Wisley, in turn produced abundant seed which was widely distributed.

C. texensis (Zone 4) (Texas, USA) represents a very distinct group of species, long ago classified botanically under the old generic name *Viorna* but now kept as a section of *Clematis*. In the British climate it behaves either as a herbaceous perennial or a sub-shrubby climber. Either way it is likely to be short-lived. It has handsome grey-green, long-stalked pinnate leaves formed of four to eight ovate leaflets. An interesting departure from the clematis norm is the lack of a terminal leaflet, its place taken by a tendril modification. In late summer and autumn, long stalked, nodding, pitcher-shaped flowers appear. Each one is about 2.5-3 cm long and, in the best forms, a soft scarlet. The four petals appear as if welded together, parting only at the slender pointed tips which recurve charmingly. This intriguing species has played its part in the evolution of the large-flowered hybrid being the main provider of the red coloration. Among the hybrid cultivars that retain something of the *texensis* charm are: 'Duchess of Albany' with tubular bell flowers of clear pink; 'Gravetye Beauty', bell-shaped, cherry-red; and 'Countess of Onslow', having bell-shaped cerise blooms, each sepal with a pale pink margin.

C. X 'The President' (Zone 6) (large-flowered hybrid) bears slightly cupped flowers to 18 cm wide, the eight sepals of a pleasing even light purple, contrasted with red-purple stamens. The plant is vigorous, clad with a mixture of simple and trifoliate leaves that are bronze-tinted when young.

C. X *triternata* (Zone 5) (*C.* X *violacea*) is a cross between *C. flammula* and *C. viticella* and comes halfway between the two but with a nod towards the latter parent. It is represented in gardens by the cultivar 'Rubromarginata', a vigorous plant bearing showers of small, fragrant white flowers each tepal margined with rosy-purple. Most nurserymen list this under *flammula*.

C. uncinata (Zone 8-9) (China) is another of that small select band of clematis species with evergreen leaves. These are divided into six to fifteen smooth ovate leaflets which are glaucous beneath. The small fragrant flowers are creamy white, freely borne in clusters in summer. In a sheltered site it can reach 4-5 m. Outside, culture in Britain is possible only in the warmest sites. In lower zones it makes a cool greenhouse plant.

C. X *vedrariensis* (Zone 6) was raised by the French nurseryman Vilmorin just prior to 1914, by crossing *C. montana rubens* with *C. chrysocoma*. Superficially it resembles a large-flowered *montana rubens*, but the leaves bear some of the pale hairs characteristic of *C. chrysocoma*. *C.* X *v.* 'Rosea' is a more richly hued cultivar.

C. veitchiana (Zone 6) (China) closely resembles *C. rehderiana* and has the same impact in the garden. The only real — or reasonably observable — difference is the bipinnate foliage.

C. verticillaris (Zone 2) (*Atragene americana*) is known as bell rue in its native North America. It is very much that country's answer to Europe's *C. alpina*, except that the leaves are trifoliate. The latter is, however, still the better garden plant if only by a short head.

C. viorna (Zone 5) (USA) is, along with *C. pitcheri*, *texensis* and others, a member of the *Viorna* group. It most resembles *C. crispa* (q.v.) but the leathery, matt red-purple sepals are shorter, to 2.5 cm. It is more or less herbaceous, generally dying back to a woody base each winter. By no means a show stopper, but interesting.

C. virginiana (Zone 4) (Virgin's bower) is eastern North America's version of old-man's-beard, *C. vitalba*, but less vigorous and with trifoliate leaves and dull white flowers. Though a nice plant to come upon in its native thickets and woods it has nothing to offer the gardener.

C. vitalba (Zone 4) (old-man's-beard, traveller's joy) ranges widely in the wild, extending through Europe to the Caucasus and south to the mountains of N Africa. It is the only clematis native to Britain and there only in England north to S Yorkshire — though naturalised elsewhere. Although very decorative in seed, its somewhat greenish-white, small flowers and extreme vigour do not make for garden worthiness. It is however, a parent of the worthwhile garden hybrid *C. X jouiniana* (q.v.). In the wild it can climb to the tops of quite tall trees; up to 30 m in height has been recorded. It is the only climber in Britain that can, in a few favoured woods produce a realistic liane!

C. viticella (Zone 4) (S Europe) is sometimes known as Virgin's bower, a name which rightly belongs to *C. virginiana* (q.v.). Known in Britain for 400 years — even a double form was grown by John Gerard, the Elizabethan gardener, prior to 1597 — it was for long the only garden clematis and a valued ornamental climber. It is a semi-woody species, much of it dying back each winter but coming up strongly each spring with stems to 4 m or so. It is, in fact, best pruned back to near ground level each late winter. The freely branching stems bear leaves of basically pinnate form, though the lowest leaflets are in turn trifoliate. From late summer to early autumn all the upper branchlets and their ramifications bear beautifully poised, nodding, red-purple to almost blue flowers. Each one is formed of four spreading sepals with very broad, rolled back tips. Several fine cultivars are available, some with a suggestion of hybridity: 'Abundance' has mauve-pink flowers with a darker vein pattern. It gained the RHS Award of Garden Merit in 1973. 'Alba Luxurians' has green-tipped white flowers and was given its AGM in 1930. 'Elegans Plena' is not, as far as I know, commercially available but may soon be. It was presumed more or less extinct until Graham Thomas discovered 'a poor wizened plant ... growing to the north of the great gates by the house' at Charlecote Park, Warwickshire. It was rescued and propagated and all plants at present in gardens have come from it. Although an ancient cultivar it is not without vigour and its fully double red flowers have fascination and charm. 'Kermesina' is wine-red and gained an AGM in 1969. 'Minuet' has creamy-white sepals edged with purple. 'Royal Velours' bears flowers of a glorious velvety purple. It was given an AM in 1948 and an AGM in 1969. 'Rubra' is a deep velvety red with a whitish eye. It has been and may still sometimes be confused with both 'Kermesina' and 'Royal Velours'.

C. X 'Vyvyan Pennell' (Zone 6) (large-flowered hybrid) is a comparative newcomer raised by the clematis specialist W.E. Pennell by crossing 'Beauty of Worcester' and 'Daniel Deronda', a semi-double blue-purple. It is one of the best of full doubles, producing 15-20 cm wide deep violet-blue flowers in summer and a bonus of single, paler-toned ones in autumn.

C. X 'W.E. Gladstone' (Zone 6) (large-flowered hybrid) bears immense lilac-blue blooms, sometimes 25 cm wide, from mid-summer to autumn.

C. X 'William Kennett' (Zone 6) (large-flowered hybrid) is not only an appealing shade of deep lavender with dark purple stamens, but the sepal margins are engagingly crimped.

Clematoclethra *Actinidiaceae*

Only three or four of the 25 known species in this largely Asiatic genus are ever seen in gardens. Although the name might suggest otherwise, they have nothing to do with either *Clematis* or *Clethra* but are close allies of *Actinidia*. The twining species described below have no fads as to soil but in zones lower than 7 need greenhouse conditions. In Britain they require sheltered sites.

C. actinidioides (Zone 8) (China) can reach 12 m or so in a tree. It has ovate to broadly lanceolate, minutely bristle-toothed leaves 4-8 cm long on long stalks. The five-petalled flowers are also long-stalked, ranging from one to several in the leaf axils. Each one is about 1.5 cm wide and white with a touch of pink. Small globose, black berries follow.

C. integrifolia (Zone 8) (China) was introduced by E.H. Wilson in 1908, but had been found previously in 1887 by the Russian explorer and botanist Grigori Potanin. It much resembles *C. actinidioides* but is a little more decorative with leaves that are glaucous beneath and bristle-toothed (a very unsatisfactory situation for a plant with this name which means uncut or smooth-edged). The flowers are white and fragrant.

C. lasioclada (Zone 7-8) (China) is also much like *C. actinidioides*, but has larger leaves, flower clusters and fruits, though not by any large amount.

C. scandens (Zone 8) (China) grows up to 7 m in height, its young shoots bearing a plentiful covering of brown bristles. The oblong-ovate to lanceolate leaves vary greatly in length from 2.5-13 cm, depending on the vigour of the stems. They are glaucous and downy beneath with bristles on the midrib both above and beneath. Small white flowers are followed by red berries.

Clianthus (parrot's bill) *Leguminosae*

Literally translated, this generic name means glory flower (Greek *kleos*, glory, and *anthos*, a flower). The name is most apt as the flowers are comparatively large, showy and strikingly shaped. There are two species, one from Australia, the other from New Zealand. Neither are true climbers but one, *C. puniceus*, can be treated as a semi-scrambler and makes fine wall decoration. In zones lower than 7 a frost-free greenhouse is needed. In most of Britain only the really sheltered sites are suitable. Almost any well drained soil is acceptable and propagation is by seeds in spring or semi-hardwood cuttings in summer.

C. puniceus (Zone 8-9) (New Zealand) has the distinction of being one of the few native New Zealand plants grown purely for ornament by the Maoris long before Europeans arrived. They call it Kowhai-ngutu-kaka and white New Zealanders have adapted this to kaka beak (the kaka is a native parrot). It is a rather thin-stemmed shrub, in shadier sites sometimes behaving as a semi-scrambler. Strong stems can reach 2-3 m or more trained on a wall, and are clad with pinnate 7-15 cm long leaves composed of up to 15 narrowly oblong leaflets. From late spring to summer, dangling clusters of giant red pea flowers illuminate the branchlets. Although basically of pea form, each 6-8 cm long bloom has a scimitar-shaped keel and an equally lengthy tapered and swept-back standard petal. The effect is both bizarre and beautiful. *C. p.* 'Albus' has creamy-white flowers; 'Roseus' covers shades of pink. Bicoloured forms are also known.

Clytostoma *Bignoniaceae*

About eight species form this tropical American genus of tendril climbers. Only the species described below is widely cultivated, thriving in sub-tropical countries where the winters are cool and mainly dry. It makes a good roof climber for the larger greenhouse requiring only a winter minimum of 7°C. Any well drained, fertile, neutral to acid soil is suitable and propagation is by stem cuttings in spring with bottom heat about 21°-24°C.

C. callistegioides (Zone 9-10) (*Bignonia callistegioides, B. speciosa*) is native to the region including southern Brazil and northern Argentina. Given the right conditions it can exceed 5 m in height but is easily curbed by late summer pruning. The evergreen leaves are formed of two elliptic, 7-10 cm long leaflets with a simple tendril of similar length between them. Depending on the temperature, flowering starts in spring or summer and carries on for several weeks. The flowers are carried in pairs which terminate short axillary shoots. Each flower is 6-9 cm long, basically of foxglove-like form but with five spreading lobes. The colour varies somewhat but is usually pale purple or lilac, the mouth and lobes with a striking pattern of rich, violet-purple veins. The inner throat shades to pale yellow. Seed pods rarely form but are intriguing, very spiny objects containing about a dozen flat, winged seeds.

Cobaea (cup and saucer creeper) *Cobaeaceae*

Only one of the 18 species in this Central and South American genus is cultivated at all widely. This is *C. scandens*, a softly woody evergreen which flowers the first year from seed and can be grown wherever summer temperatures exceed 18°-20°C. Ordinary fertile soil and a sunny site are needed. Propagation is by seeds sown in early to mid-spring, ideally singly in small pots at 18°-20°C.

    C. scandens (Zone 9) is also known as monastery bells and Mexican ivy. Botanical reference works seem undecided as to the exact range of this species, but it appears to be wild in Mexico south to northern Chile. It probably well exceeds 15 m in the wild, and even as an annual it can reach 4-5 m. The leaves are pinnate, composed of four to six ovate to elliptic leaflets, each to 10 cm long, and terminated by an elaborately branched tendril. The latter is worthy of close examination, especially in the way it works. Each thread-like branch has a minutely hooked tip. Wafted by the wind, these hooks can catch on to a support and the tendril branches then fold around it. Later, the main part of the tendril spirals like a spring, pulling the stem closer to its support. The large, long-stalked bell flowers arise from the upper leaf axils. They are 6-8 cm long, opening yellow-green then steadily changing to purple. In *C. s.* 'Alba' the flowers are greenish-white. The calyx is bright green, five-lobed and waved and only fancifully like a saucer. As an annual it flowers from late summer until the first frost; under glass, from spring to early winter.

Cocculus *Menispermaceae*

Very few of the eleven species of climbers and shrubs in this genus are cultivated. Many are tropical but not showy enough to merit greenhouse space. Those described here are hardy in Britain. They are woody climbers with tiny six-petalled, dioecious flowers followed by coloured berries. Ordinary, but not dry, soil and sheltered partial shade is their cultural requirement. Propagation is by seed when ripe, root cuttings in late winter and stem cuttings in late summer.

chizandra grandiflora rubriflora

Sandersonia aurantiaca

uonymus fortunei radicans

Eccremocarpus scaber

◀ *Lapageria rosea*
'Nashcourt'

▶ *Clematis viticella*
'Minuet'

◀ *Hydrangea petiolaris*

▶ *Wistaria floribunda*
'Issai'

Clematis florida bicolor

Clematis cirrhosa balearica

C. carolinus (Zone 5) (coral beads, red-berried moon seed) is native to moist woods and thickets in south eastern USA. It climbs to about 4 m, the slim stems clad with deciduous, ovate, entire or variously lobed leaves to 10 cm long. The insignificant greenish flowers are in panicles up to 13 cm long. Showy, glistening red pea-sized berries follow.

C. trilobus (Zone 5) (E. Asia) has a similar appearance to *C. carolinus* the ovate, sometimes shallowly three-lobed leaves up to 13 cm long. The flowers and fruit are in smaller clusters, the latter black with a waxy white patina.

Codonopsis (bonnet bellflower) *Campanulaceae*

Among the 30 or more species in this Asiatic genus are annuals and perennials, some of the latter with twining stems and a true climbing habit. They are herbaceous, dying back to a tuberous rootstock annually. The usually simple leaves are alternate and the one to several flowers are terminal, nodding or inclined and much like those of the true bellflowers (*Campanula*). Ordinary moisture retentive, but well-drained, soil is suitable and a site in partial shade or sun. Propagation is by seeds in spring or when ripe, careful division when possible in spring just as the new shoots show, and cuttings of young shoots when 5-7.5 cm long placed in sand in a propagating case.

C. convolvulacea (Zone 8) (Himalayas, western China) can achieve 2 m or more in height but is often less. The stems are very slender with usually only a few branches. The leaves are ovate to lanceolate, entire or coarsely toothed, up to 7 cm long. Strong stems bear several long-stalked flowers in an open cluster in late summer. Each bloom is about 5 cm wide and opens out almost flat with five broad lobes. Violet-blue is the usual colour but it varies in intensity from plant to plant. *C. c.* 'Alba' is white. In Britain at least, this species needs a sheltered site with its head in the sun and is most effective roaming through a wall shrub. *C. c. forrestii* (*C. tibetica*) is somewhat more robust with larger leaves and flowers.

C. tangshen (Zone 7-8) (western China) climbs to 3 m with ovate, sparsely crenate-toothed leaves 3-6 cm long. The 4 cm long flowers are beautifully bell-shaped, chartreuse green, patterned inside with purple stripes and spots. It could be splendid climbing up a wall-trained *Artemisia arborescens*. Often short lived it will not stand prolonged hard frost.

C. vinciflora (Zone 8-9) (Tibet) is much like a smaller version of *C. convolvulacea* and is sometimes amalgamated with that species. It grows to about 1.5 m with 4 cm wide purple to lilac-blue flowers. Even in zone 8 it needs a very sheltered site out of doors. Neutral to acid soil is necessary for success.

C. viridiflora (Zone 7-8) (Central to E. Asia) is rather akin to

C. tangshen but smaller in all its parts, growing up to about 1.5 m.

Convolvulus *Convolvulaceae*

This large and cosmopolitan genus of 250 species contains annuals, perennials and shrubs, most species in these categories being twining climbers, but not all. Apart from the popular non-climbing annual *C. tricolor*, few species are grown in temperate countries. The two described here need sharply drained soil and a sheltered, sunny site. When happily established they can become invasive and it might be as well to contain the wandering underground stems with slates or tiles inserted vertically in the soil around each plant. Propagation is by division or seeds in spring or cuttings in early summer.

C. althaeoides (Zone 8) (Mediterranean region) both trails and twines, much depending on available supports. Even when the latter are present, the young growth each spring often seems to prefer to trail at first; the plant then goes up to about 1 m in height, occasionally almost twice this. The grey-green leaves are ovate-cordate, the basal ones toothed or shallowly lobed, the upper ones deeply fingered. From summer to autumn the upper leaf axils bear one to three very widely funnel-shaped purple-rose flowers, each one 3-4 cm across.

C. elegantissimus (Zone 8) (eastern Mediterranean) has been known as *C. tenuissimus* and is much like *C. althaeoides* but bears a closely pressed coating of glistening, silky silvery hairs and has solitary flowers. A most decorative plant, especially when rambling over low shrubs such as *Cistus* or *Genista* species.

Cucurbita (gourds, squashes etc.) *Cucurbitaceae*

This tropical and sub-tropical genus of 25 species contains the well known marrow, pumpkin, summer squash and ornamental gourd. Although largely grown for their edible fruits all are handsome tendril climbers and ideal for covering unsightly areas and garden buildings. Their big leaves make good summer ground cover. They have long-stalked, rounded, more or less lobed leaves and unisexual flowers. The latter are borne singly in the leaf axils and are large and showy. The female flowers have an embryo fruit just behind the petals and a short stalk. The males lack the fruit and are long-stalked. To be sure of fruits, hand pollination is recommended. The operation is simplicity itself. The male flower is picked, the petal lobes stripped away and the club-like mass of stamens used like a brush onto the crown-like stigma of the female flower. Rich soil is required, both moisture retentive and well drained, and a place in the sun. Supports must be strong to take the considerable weight of the fruit. Propagation is by seeds sown singly in 7.5-9 cm pots in spring under glass at about 21°C.

C. pepo (Zone 5 — annual) (Mexico and south western USA) contains the most ornamental forms and cultivars including the familiar marrow and the bitter, inedible, ornamental gourds. The latter is botanically *C. p. ovifera*, a climber to 3 m or more with well developed branching tendrils, large bright yellow marrow-like flowers and small hard-shelled fruits in a variety of shapes often startlingly bicoloured yellow and green, or mottled or striped, the skin smoothed or warted. They dry and retain their colour well and make intriguing ornaments.

Decumaria *Hydrangeaceae*

D

Two species of root climbers comprise this genus, one deciduous from the USA, the other evergreen from China. They are closely allied to *Hydrangea* and have opposite pairs of simple leaves and clusters of small flowers formed of seven to ten narrow petals. Ordinary fertile, moisture retentive soil is suitable, ideally in sheltered half-shade. Propagation is by cuttings in late summer.

D. barbara (Zone 8, lower in US) (south eastern USA) grows up to 10 m or more in height with deciduous, ovate, glossy leaves 7-13 cm long. The white flower clusters are erect, 5-7.5 cm long and wide, opening in summer. It needs a warm, very sheltered site.

D. sinensis (Zone 7) (China) weaves a substantial layer of slender stems and somewhat lustrous, slightly yellowish-green, ovate leaves up to 9 cm long. The summer-borne flowers are cream, in clusters 5-9 cm high. This neglected species makes an uncommon and pleasing wall cover and should be tried more often.

Dichelostemma *Alliaceae*

The six species in this genus of cormous plants from western N. America were formerly placed in the much larger *Brodiaea*. Except the one species described here, all have strap-shaped, almost grassy leaves and erect, naked flowering stems topped by an umbel of six-tepalled, starry to bell-shaped flowers. They need well drained soil and a sunny site, and a frost-free greenhouse in zones below 8. Propagation is by seeds in spring or removing offsets during the dormant season. The corms should be potted or planted in autumn and protected from severe frost.

D. volubilis (Zone 8) (snake lily, twining brodiaea) is restricted to the inner coast ranges of California, from Tehama to Solano Counties. There it is found on bushy and open slopes in both rocky and clay soils. It has leaves up to 60 cm or more in length and a flowering stem 90-150 cm long. It is this stem which is the surprise for it twines and loops through the bushes to bring the cluster of drooping or spreading pink flowers into the sun. Each flower is about 1.5 cm wide, with an inflated tubular base, and opens in summer.

Dioscorea *Dioscoreaceae*

Approximately 600 species are listed in this genus of twining, tuberous-rooted plants from the tropics and sub-tropics. Most of the cultivated species are food plants, providing the yams of commerce. Only *D. elephantipes* is widely grown as an ornamental. It needs semi-desert conditions and, in Britain, greenhouse protection. A sharply drained soil and plenty of sun are basic requirements. A winter minimum of 5°-7°C is adequate. The stems come up annually and during growth the plant needs regular watering. From autumn to the following spring it must be kept dry. Propagation is by seed in spring or cuttings in summer of stems that are mature and firm.

   D. elephantipes (Zone 9-10) (elephant's foot) (S Africa) is still much better known under its earlier name *Testudinaria elephantipes*. It has a large, semi-globose pyramidal tuber at least half of which is above the ground; this upper part is covered with curious polygonal, corky knobs. The aerial stems reach 2-3 m and bear heart to kidney-shaped leaves and racemes of small, greenish six-tepalled flowers in summer. It is also known as tortoise plant and Hottentot bread, the latter name referring to its use as a famine food. The tubers contain saponins and are only just edible.

Dipladenia, see *Mandevilla*.

Distictis (Zone 9) (Mexican blood flower) *Bignoniaceae*

One species, formerly classified in *Bignonia, Phaedranthus* and *Pithecoctenum*, comprises this Mexican genus. *D. buccinatoria* is a tendril climber to 5 m or so with compound leaves formed of two long-stalked ovate leaflets 5-9 cm long and a terminal 3-branched tendril. Often more or less pendent, the slenderly trumpet-shaped five-lobed flowers are up to 12 cm long and carried in terminal clusters. They are deep rose-crimson, the tube orange-yellow within, and open in late spring and summer. Fertile soil and plenty of sun are the primary requirements for a good floral display. Propagation is by cuttings of short side shoots in early summer.

Dolichos (hyacinth bean) *Leguminosae*

Only one of the 70 species in this genus is much grown as an ornamental. This is *D. lablab* (Zone 9, or 5 as annual) (*Lablab niger, L. vulgaris*), variously known as Egyptian, Indian or hyacinth bean. A short-lived twining perennial, or grown in temperate countries as a half-hardy annual, it superficially resembles a runner bean (*Phaseolus* q.v.). Twining upwards to a height of 3-5 m it has trifoliate leaves

about 15 cm or more long and showy purple or white pea flowers
in axillary racemes to 30 cm long. The pods are 5-15 cm long,
flattened, often purple-flushed, containing rounded, flattened beans
which can vary from white to buff or reddish, brown or black. Both
the immature pods and dried beans are eaten in tropical countries,
especially in India.

Figure 5.11
*Doxantha
unguis-cati*

Doxantha (cat's-claw vine) *Bignoniaceae*

Only one of the two species in this genus is commonly cultivated, *D.
unguis-cati* (Zone 8-9), a typical bignonia climber with ingenious
claw-tipped tendrils. Capable of reaching 10 m or more in height, it
has opposite pairs of leaves, each one formed of two lance-shaped,
slender pointed leaflets. Between the leaflets are three short, straight
tendrils with small but incredibly fine-pointed hooks capable of
catching into the tiniest cracks and crevices. The flowers are bright
yellow, up to 10 cm wide and with a 4 cm long tubular base bearing

orange lines within. They open in the upper leaf axils in late spring and summer. Ordinary soil is suitable and propagation is easy by summer cuttings.

Dregea, see *Wattakaka*.

E

Eccremocarpus (Chilean glory flower) *Bignoniaceae*

Five species of evergreen tendril climbers form this western S American genus, but only one is grown. *E. scaber* (Zone 8-9) is a native of the drier parts of Chile where it seldom seems to reach its potential of floriferousness and height. Nevertheless, it can be a memorable sight in its homeland. I still clearly remember a day's plant collecting in the coastal range of central Chile. Most of the day had been spent in the futile pursuit of the rare Chilean crocus (*Tecophilaea cyanocrocus*) but finally I decided to cut across country back to the landrover. The track lost itself in a rocky gully largely overgrown with scrub through which I fought my way, getting steadily hotter, crosser and more weary. It also seemed that I was more or less lost. Then, during a pause to look around, I saw flights of tubular orange flowers just above my head. It was the familiar glory flower which we had not previously seen wild, and it made my day. Soon afterwards a clearer track appeared and from then on the going was better. In Britain this eccremocarpus is a short-lived woody perennial to 4 m or more. In hard winters it is killed, or cut to ground level. However, raised from seed in warmth in early spring it can be treated as a half-hardy annual. The leaves are bipinnate, the tips with elaborately branched tendrils. The tubular flowers are 2-3 cm long, obliquely bottle-shaped, orange-red and opening from summer to late autumn. *E. s. aureus* is yellow, *E. s. carmineus*, carmine-red.

Ercilla *Phytolaccaceae*

This genus of two S American evergreen root climbers is fairly rare in cultivation but one, *E. volubilis* (Zone 8-9) (*E. spicata*, *Bridgesia spicata*) is sometimes met with. Although very modest in appearance it can closely clothe a wall or tree trunk with a very pleasing tapestry of oval, deep green, pale-veined leaves. Wandering through a tree as it so often does in its temperate rain forest home, the effect is very different. The stems push along the smaller branches until there is no more room, then arch outwards and downwards into space. These hanging tips provide most of the flowers; small, bell-like and whitish, in short, dense spikes from every leaf axil. The main climbing stems can scale trees to 6 m or more, but it is easily kept much lower by pruning in spring. It is very tolerant as to soil, but needs partial shade and shelter from cold winds. Propagation is by stem cuttings in late summer or layering in spring.

88

Euonymus *Celastraceae*

Among the 170 or so species of trees and shrubs in this genus is one very useful climbing species, *E. fortunei* (Zone 5) (*E. japonicus acutus*, *E. radicans acutus*) from Japan, Korea and China. It is a root climber in the manner of ivy, with alternate pairs of elliptic to ovate, glossy evergreen leaves. The flowers are small and greenish-white and are carried only on the non-climbing branches which form when the plant reaches the top of its support, a situation exactly comparable to that of ivy. The fruits are pea sized, berry-like pinkish capsules that split open to disclose orange seeds. Any ordinary soil is suitable and a position in shade or sun. Propagation is by cuttings in late summer and autumn. Several distinct cultivars are available. *E. f. radicans* is the most vigorous form, growing to 8 m or more in height, with elliptic leaves 3-4 cm long and usually greenish-white fruits. In *E. f. r.* 'Colorata' the leaves take on rich shades of red-purple in winter. 'Variegatus' has larger leaves strikingly bordered with white. 'Argenteo-marginata' and 'Gracilis' are alternative names, used particularly in Europe.

Eustrephus (wombat berry) (*Philesiaceae* (*Liliaceae*))

The solitary species in this genus is *E. latifolius* (Zone 8-9), a native of the extreme east of Australia where it appears in a variety of habitats where the soil is reasonably moist. It is one of those climbers which is hard to categorise, having no means of holding on. The stems are flexuous, however, and it behaves most like a scrambler attaining several metres in height. The narrowly ovate, glossy evergreen leaves are about 8 cm long and alternately borne. In their upper axils are carried small clusters of six-tepalled starry, pink to pale purple flowers about 12-15 mm wide. A close look at a single bloom is very worthwhile. The three outer sepals are smooth, contrasting greatly with the three inner ones which are covered with long, white, woolly kinky hairs. In zones 8 and below this is a plant for a frost-free greenhouse. Propagation is by seed in spring.

X Fatshedera *Araliaceae*

This bigeneric hybrid gets an honourable mention namely because one parent is an ivy. It was raised by the French nursery firm Lizé Frères of Nantes in 1910 by crossing *Fatsia japonica* 'Moseri' and *Hedera helix hibernica* and named X *F. lizei* (Zone 7). It lacks the climbing roots of ivy and behaves somewhat like a scrambler. Its main use is in clothing shady, low walls and tree stumps to 2 m and it needs tying to its support. The evergreen leaves are 10-25 cm long and wide, deeply five-lobed, rich green and glossy. The flowers are rather like those of ivy, but sterile. X *F. l.* 'Variegata' has leaves with an irregular white margin. Culture as for *Hedera*.

F

Ficus (fig) *Moraceae*

No less than 800 species of trees, shrubs and climbers form this widespread, largely tropical and sub-tropical genus. Only one climber, *F. pumila* (Zone 9) (*F. repens*) will stand a slight touch of frost and even in zone 8 needs a warm site. It is a root climber to 4 m or more which behaves like ivy. In the early years it has very slender stems and small ovate leaves 1-2.5 cm long. When old enough, but only after it has reached the top of its support (1 m is high enough), it produces non-climbing branches bearing longer leaves up to 10 cm and pear-shaped figs. The latter develop only in mild climates or under glass. In Britain it grows outside in the Tresco Abbey Gardens, Isles of Scilly, but generally needs a greenhouse. It thrives splendidly in Madeira, and in North Island, New Zealand, is used as a hedging plant. A low wall or fence is erected, and the young ficus growth covers it with a dense web of tightly adhering stems, then throws out mature branches which are clipped to shape. Any well-drained soil is suitable and a site in sun or partial shade, even fairly heavy shade, in warm conditions. Propagation is by cuttings in summer.

G

Gelsemium (false jasmine) *Loganiaceae*

One of the two species that forms this genus is fairly popular in frost-free countries and makes an attractive cool greenhouse plant. This is *Gelsemium sempervirens* (Zone 8-9, Zone 7 in USA) from south eastern USA, where it is known as evening trumpet flower, and from Mexico to Guatemala. It inhabits dry to wet woods and thickets. Reaching to 6 m in the wild but seldom much above half this in cultivation, it is a twining evergreen with glossy, narrow leaves to 5 cm long and axillary and terminal clusters of deep to pale yellow flowers in summer. Each flower is about 3 cm long, trumpet-shaped with five rounded petal lobes, and exhales a sweet scent. It needs fertile, well-drained but not dry soil and a sunny or partially shaded site. In Britain it needs a greenhouse. Where the growth is thoroughly ripened by a long, hot summer it will stand a fair bit of winter cold. Propagation is by cuttings in summer, or seed in spring at 18°-21°C.

Gloriosa (glory lily) *Liliaceae*

Bearing the Latin name for glorious, this genus of five or six species from Africa has no difficulty in upholding such a superlative epithet. The three best species are described here. All spring from curious, cylindrical V-shaped tubers. Growth starts in spring, flowering takes place in summer and the plant dies back to a new tuber in autumn. Tubers must be stored dry at not less than 7°C. If started under glass in pots in spring they can be planted out in all areas with a reasonably warm summer. In Britain they are best in a greenhouse but will grow

90

outside in very wind-sheltered sites. Any ordinary soil is suitable. Propagation is by seeds in spring, or offset tubers at re-planting time.

G. carsonii (Zone 9) (central Africa) is rather like a small version of *G. rothschildiana* but only about half the height, with 6-7.5 cm wide flowers composed of strongly reflexed, waved purple-red tepals shading to yellow at the base.

G. rothschildiana (Zone 9) (tropical Africa) is the tallest species to 2.5 m, at least in cultivation. It is much like *G. superba* but has crimson flowers, the base of each wavy tepal margined yellow on opening, then ageing red.

G. simplex (Zone 9) (*G. virescens*) (tropical Africa) reaches about 1.2 m in height with flowers starting green then maturing yellow to orange-red.

G. superba (Zone 9) (tropical Africa and Asia) is perhaps the most commonly grown species (often listed as *rothschildiana*) and provides the basic description of habit and flower shape for all species. Indeed, the botanist D.V. Field, who has studied this genus in the wild, considers that all the so-called species would be best classified as varieties of this one species. Each tuber produces an erect slim stem clad with lance-shaped glossy leaves that taper to a fine tail-like point tipped by a small hook (see also page 15). The stem may branch near the top and from each of the upper leaf axils arises a long stalk at a 45° angle at the end of which is poised most elegantly a nodding Turk's-cap lily-like flower, in this case about 8-9 cm wide. The yellow ageing to red tepals are both waved and crimped.

Hardenbergia *Leguminosae*

H

The two Australian species in this genus are neglected in British greenhouses, thriving in a minimum temperature of 5°C and providing showers of charming little pea flowers in early spring. They grow in ordinary soil in sun or light shade and are easily propagated by seeds in spring or cuttings in late summer.

H. comptoniana (Zone 9) (Western Australia) is known in its native land as 'sarsaparilla' (a name applied to several other plants in N America). It has a profusion of slender, wiry stems set with leaves composed of three to five ovate to lanceolate leaflets each one 5-10 cm long, and axillary racemes 7-13 cm long of small violet-blue flowers.

H. violacea (Zone 9) (Eastern Australia) is similar to the previous species, but has simple leaves and usually darker flowers though pink and white forms exist.

Hedera (ivy) *Araliaceae*

Depending on the botanical authority there are five to fifteen wild species of ivy and quite literally hundreds of cultivated varieties.

Between them they provide some of the most decorative and satisfying of all foliage climbers. All are self-clinging by very efficient aerial roots. All head straight up their supports and, on reaching the top, produce non-clinging branches with usually different shaped leaves and tiny greenish flowers in spherical clusters during the autumn. The berries are generally black, but in a few cases are yellow. Ordinary soil is suitable and the whole range of exposure from utter deep shade to full sun. Propagation is by cuttings from late summer to early spring.

H. canariensis (Zone 7-8) (Canary Islands to Azores and NW Africa) has red-flushed stems and leaf stalks and unlobed ovate leaves 10-15 cm long. The usual form seen is glossy, but matt green forms occur. In Britain at least, this species is largely represented by 'Gloire de Marengo', with irregularly creamy-white leaf margins and greyish patches on the upper surface. Although a highly popular and successful house plant, as garden ornament it is totally inferior to *H. colchica* 'Dentata Variegata' (q.v.). 'Ravensholst' is the finest green-leaved cultivar, with larger leaves − up to 20 cm long − with two short side-lobes which give the leaves a broad-shouldered look. It is hardier than other forms of *canariensis*.

H. colchica (Zone 5) (Caucasus to northern Iran) is the so-called Persian ivy and the largest leaved and most handsome of all ivies for clothing a wall or tall tree stump. It can climb up to at least 15 m and has thick-textured heart-shaped leaves to 25 cm long. The form most frequently seen is 'Dentata' with leaf margins bearing a few scattered teeth. 'Dentata Variegata' is the most striking of all variegated ivies, each leaf being boldly margined creamy yellow and with a greyish zone between it and the dark centre. 'Sulphur Heart' ('Paddy's Pride') has an irregular yellow centre to each leaf or a pale to yellow-green area with yellow veins.

H. helix (Zone 5) (Europe to the Caucasus) is the common ivy, ubiquitous as a wild plant in Britain and the parent of hundreds of cultivars. The typical wild plant, if such there is in this very variable species, can climb to 30 m, with three to five-lobed leaves 4-10 cm across, usually deep green and glossy. The leaves on the flowering branches are generally ovate and unlobed. The following cultivars are very much a personal selection from among the many available. For the rest a good specialist nursery catalogue should be consulted. See also the book *Ivies* by Peter Q. Rose, Blandford Press, 1980. *H. h. baltica* is an ordinary looking ivy selected for its extreme hardiness and suitability for N American gardens. 'Buttercup' is one of the brightest and most desirable of ivies for garden use, having bright yellow-green leaves, richer in tone when grown in bright light. 'Deltoidea' has bluntly triangular leaves with the two rounded basal lobes overlapping. It is sometimes known as shield ivy and is slow growing and very distinct. 'Digitata' has been listed in nurserymen's catalogues for at least 150 years. It is distinguished by the long, slender pointed five-lobed leaves. 'Glacier' has been a popular house plant for about 30 years and is also good in the garden with its basically three-lobed, grey-green and silvery patched leaves with or without a narrow cream border. 'Goldheart' ('Jubilee') bears an apt name, each small, entire to three-lobed leaf centrally splashed with bright yellow. It is justly popular as both wall covering and ground cover. 'Hibernica' (Irish ivy) is, in Britain at least, commonly seen in churchyards and was formerly much planted in gardens. It is a tetraploid form with thick-textured, rather larger leaves that are wider than their length — up to 15 cm. 'Manda's Crested' arose as a mutant in the nursery of W.A. Manda Inc., New Jersey, USA and was described in 1940. Curiously and attractively wavy leaved it has the bonus of becoming red suffused in winter. Not a good climber but worth tying in now and then. 'Pedata' (bird's foot ivy) has leaves with five narrow lobes, the centre one by far the longest. They are dark green with whitish veins. 'Purpurea' turns a bronze-purple in winter.

H. napaulensis (Zone 7) (Himalayas) can reach the tops of quite tall trees in its native land, but it is not much grown in Britain and recent introductions by Roy Lancaster and others have not yet proved themselves. The leaves are most distinctive, ovate to lanceolate with somewhat irregular, smallish forward pointing lobes. The fruit is orange-yellow but so far has not been produced in Britain. It is less hardy than *H. helix*.

H. rhombea (Zone 6) (Japan, Korea, Taiwan) is the so-called Japanese ivy with very leathery-textured, deep green heart-shaped leaves to 5 cm long. Some leaves may have one or two small basal lobes. The fruits are black. *H. r.* 'Variegata' has the leaves narrowly white rimmed.

Hibbertia *Dilleniaceae*

About 100 species of shrubs and climbers comprise this genus. Most of them are Australian, but the rest range from Malagasy to the islands of the western Pacific. Those described here have simple leaves and single rose-like flowers. They thrive in ordinary, ideally humus-rich, neutral soil in sun or partial shade. Propagation is by cuttings in summer or seeds in spring.

H. dentata (Zone 9) (Queensland to eastern Victoria) inhabits mainly moist forest, often among eucalyptus. It has slender pinkish stems to 3 m or so and dark green, narrowly ovate leaves with well-spaced teeth. The clear yellow flowers are 2.5-4 cm wide and appear in spring and summer.

H. scandens (Zone 9) (*H. volubilis*) (Queensland, New South

93

Wales) is the showiest and most vigorous of the cultivated species. Although it often trails on the ground in the wild, it can also twine upwards to 5 m or more. The young shoots and leaf undersides are silky-hairy, the latter narrow and up to 10 cm long. Throughout much of the year, rich yellow 5 cm wide flowers expand at the tips of short leafy lateral shoots.

Holboellia *Lardizabalaceae*

The ten species in this genus are closely related to *Stauntonia* (q.v.), having the same characteristics and cultural requirements. In *Stauntonia* the stamens are united, in *Holboellia* they are separate; a small character upon which to found a genus.

H. coriacea (Zone 7) (*Stauntonia coriacea*) (China) was introduced from Hupeh by E.H. Wilson in 1907. It is a vigorous twiner to 6 m or so, with ribbed stems and trifoliate leaves. The leaflets are more or less lance-shaped, long-pointed, deeply toothed and lustrous. Seedling plants usually have rounded leaves and take some time before they start to climb properly. The flowers open in late spring and are unisexual. Male flowers are 1 cm long, white with purple stalks and are borne in terminal clusters. The females are larger, in the lower leaf axils, greenish-white, delicately flushed purple. Purple, pod-like fleshy fruits up to 7 cm long follow, each containing a number of coal black seeds.

H. latifolia (Zone 8) (Himalayas) reached Britain as long ago as 1840 but has never been much grown, probably because of its half-hardy nature. In most respects it is very much like *H. coriacea* and some botanists would unite the two under the *latifolia* name. Sometimes this species has three to seven leaflets and the flowers are more sweetly fragrant. The somewhat longer, plumper fruits are edible.

Hoya (wax flower) *Asclepiadaceae*

Depending on the botanical authority there are between 70 and 200 species in this widespread tropical genus. Most of the species are twining and root-clinging climbers with fleshy leaves in pairs, and pendent umbels of thick, waxy-petalled, starry flowers. One species, *H. carnosa*, will stand cool conditions down to 4°C in winter if kept dry, and makes a splendid troublefree plant for a barely heated greenhouse. It thrives best in peaty, leafy soil but will grow in any proprietary compost. Propagation is by cuttings in summer.

H. carnosa (Zone 9) (southern China to northern Australia) is the common wax plant or flower, a twiner to 4 m or more with lustrous ovate to obovate leaves which are thick and fleshy but have a firm leathery skin. Neat, rounded umbels of up to 50 or more flowers appear from the summer to late autumn. The axillary stalks which bear them produce several crops of flowers often over a period of two or more years, a fairly unique feature among flowering plants of all kinds. The waxy, pink-flushed, flattened pentagonal buds resemble cake decorations or buttons and open to a double five-pointed pale pink star with a crimson eye. A strong, all-pervading fragrance is exhaled during the evening and night.

Humulus (hop) *Cannabidaceae*

Two species of herbaceous perennial twiners form this genus. They have pairs of three to seven-lobed, maple-like leaves and tiny dioecious, petalless greenish flowers. The female flowers shelter behind broad overlapping bracts clustered together in cone-like spikes which provide the hops of commerce. Any ordinary fertile, reasonably moist soil is suitable, and though shade tolerant the best effect is in sun. Propagation is by seeds or cuttings of basal shoots in spring. Sown under glass in early spring they can be grown as annuals.

H. japonicus (Zone 6) (Japanese hop) comes from temperate eastern Asia, not just Japan. It climbs to about 6 m each season and has five to seven-lobed leaves up to 12 cm long and wide. In 'Variegatus' they are splashed and streaked white.

H. lupulus (Zone 6) (*H. americanus*) is the common or European hop but has a wide range in the wild, spanning the northern temperate zone. It is much like *H. japonicus*, but the leaves are three to five-lobed and up to 15 cm long. *H. l.* 'Aureus' has leaves which are flushed golden yellow; it is a pleasing plant to brighten up a dull wall or shrubbery.

Hydrangea *Hydrangeaceae*

Botanists seem undecided as to how many species there are in this genus; some give as low as 23, others 80. Only a few of these are climbers, the rest shrubs and small trees. The climbers cling by roots and have pairs of entire leaves and flattened rather lacy heads of tiny four to five-petalled fertile flowers surrounded by larger sterile ones. They grow in ordinary soil, ideally in partial shade, but tolerate full sun. Propagation is by layering in spring or heel cuttings in late summer.

H. anomala (Zone 4) (Himalayas, China) is deciduous and climbs to at least 15 m. The toothed, ovate leaves are 7-15 cm long, sometimes more in shaded sheltered sites. Around mid-summer, 15-20 cm wide floral corymbs expand, the cream fertile flowers tiny, the white sterile ones 2-4 cm wide. In Britain at least, this hydrangea is mainly represented by *H. a. petiolaris*, better known simply as *H. petiolaris*. This has smaller, more finely toothed leaves and flatter corymbs of white fertile flowers and slightly larger sterile ones. In the wild it is restricted to Japan, there reaching the tops of trees 24 m tall. In the garden it is best on a shady wall or a tall tree stump; on a living tree

95

its floral display is largely lost to sight.

H. serratifolia (Zone 8) (Chile, Argentina) is the highly inappropriate name for the better known *H. integerrima*. The two names are opposites — with teeth, and without. In the wild, however, the plant is variable, some specimens having toothless leaves, others toothed, with a complete range of in-betweens. It is evergreen and in the temperate rain forests of southern Chile presents quite a spectacle climbing in some areas to the tops of all the trees. The dark green leaves are somewhat glossy, 6-15 cm long, and make an excellent foil for the fluffy clusters of creamy white flowers which open in late summer. It received the RHS Award of Merit in 1952 and deserves to be tried much more often, being generally hardier than often stated.

I

Ipomoea (morning glory) *Convolvulaceae*

No less than 500 species are embraced under this generic name. Not all are climbers, some being erect annuals, perennials and shrubs. The climbers are twiners, mostly with ovate, sometimes lobed leaves and funnel to trumpet-shaped flowers. They need fertile, ideally humus-rich, soil and a warm sunny site. Propagation is by seeds (pre-soaked in tepid water for twelve hours), ideally sown singly in 6.5-7.5 cm pots at 21°-24°C in spring. When seedlings show the first true leaf, the temperature can be reduced to a minimum of 15°C.

I. acuminata (Zone 9) (*I. learii*, *Pharbitis learii*) is the blue dawn flower from tropical America. It is much grown and naturalised in warm countries. In North Island, New Zealand, for example, it is a lovely sight covering trees and shrubs by the roadside, but its growth is dense and a menace to the indigenous vegetation. It is a more or less evergreen perennial growing to 6 m or so with broadly ovate, sometimes three-lobed, leaves. In summer it bears in profusion rich purple-blue flowers ageing reddish-pink, each up to 10 cm wide.

I. bona-nox (Zone 9, Zone 5 as annual) (*I. alba*, *I. noctiflora*, *Calonyction aculeatum*) probably originated in tropical America but is now much naturalised throughout the tropics. Popularly known as moonflower, it is a vigorous perennial to 5 m. The leaves are ovate to rounded, sometimes three-lobed, up to 20 cm long. Stalked clusters of buds arise in the upper leaf axils but usually only one opens at a time. The scented white flowers expand in the evening, each one opening out flat to 12 cm wide. A well-grown plant in full bloom is worth going out of one's way to see. In Britain it needs a warm summer to perform well.

I. coccinea (Zone 5) (*Quamoclit coccinea*) (south eastern USA) is the red morning glory which can so startingly light up thickets and waste places by the roadside of its home country. It is an annual with ovate-cordate leaves which can be entire or bear large teeth or

96

small lobes. The scarlet, yellow-throated flowers have 4 cm long tubes and are carried in stalked clusters from the leaf axils during the late summer to autumn period.

I. hederacea (Zone 5) (*Pharbitis hederacea*) (Tropical America) is similar to and much confused with *I. nil* but has short, broad sepals abruptly contracted to very slender, spreading or recurved tips.

I. nil (Zone 9, Zone 5 as annual) (*Pharbitis nil*) may originally have come from southern USA but has now spread throughout the tropics. Behaving as either an annual or a perennial, it has broadly ovate-cordate leaves, usually shallowly three-lobed and up to 15 cm wide. The flowers are 5 cm wide in shades of purple, pink, red and

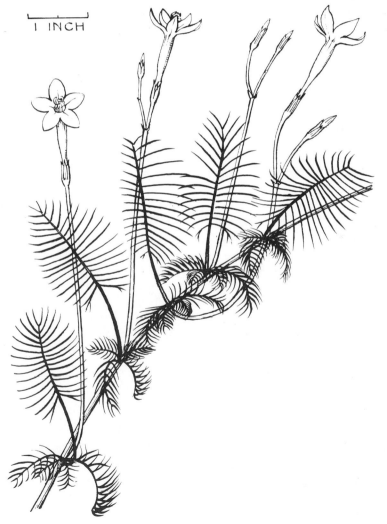

I INCH

Figure 5.12
Ipomoea quamoclit

blue. The popular cultivar 'Scarlett O'Hara' with crimson flowers belongs to this species, as does the large, double-flowered strain known as Imperial Japanese (*I. imperialis* of gardens). It is distinguished from the very similar *I. hederacea* by its lanceolate sepals with slender tips.

I. lobata, see *Mina lobata*.

I. purpurea (Zone 5) (*Pharbitis purpurea*) (tropical America) is naturalised in the drier parts of the tropics and is closely akin to *I. nil* and *hederacea*. It is the best known of the morning glories. Unlike *I. hederacea* and *nil* it always has unlobed, ovate-cordate leaves and the sepals of the flowers are broadly lanceolate with fairly abrupt points. White, pink, magenta and purple-blue forms are grown, the cultivar 'Violacea' being double. *I. p. diversifolia* (*I.*

Figure 5.13
Ipomoea tricolor

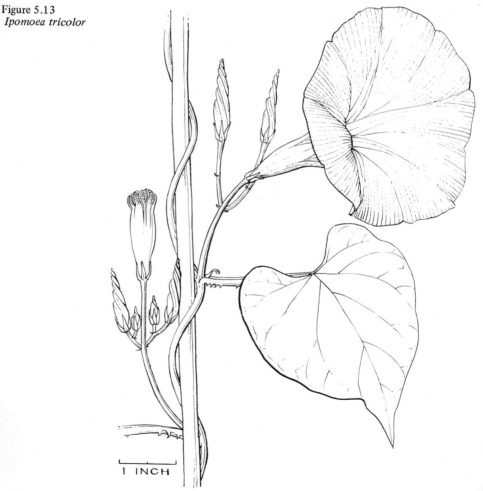

I INCH

98

mexicana) has a mixture of entire and three to five-lobed leaves on the same plant.

I. quamoclit (Zone 5) (*Quamoclit pennata*) (cypress vine) occurs around the tropics, largely as a weed. It is, though, a beautiful weed with its pinnate leaves cut into thread-like segments and slender-tubed 4 cm long scarlet flowers. A slender annual to 3 m or more, it is quite unlike any other cultivated *Ipomoea*. It is a pity that the old species synonym *pennata* (meaning 'feathered') cannot be used as it so aptly describes the foliage.

I. tricolor (Zone 5) (*I. rubrocaerulea*) originates in Mexico and adjacent tropical American countries, and is widely cultivated in warm countries elsewhere. It is a robust annual to 4 m or more in rich soil and with plenty of warmth. Smooth and hairless through-out, the well-branched stems bear ovate-cordate, slender-tipped leaves to 10 cm long. The purplish-blue flowers are large and showy, to 10 cm wide and long. Best known is the rich sky blue 'Heavenly Blue'. 'Blue Star' and 'Summer Skies' are light sky blue, while 'Flying Saucers' is striped rich blue and white. White and pink cultivars are available.

Jasminum (jasmine) *Oleaceae*

Most of the 200-300 species in this genus of shrubs and climbers are tropical. The best known species have trifoliate or pinnate leaves and the typical primrose-like flower formed of a slender tube and five to six flatly spreading petal lobes. The fruit is a black, berry-like drupe with a single large seed. Ordinary soil is suitable and a sunny to partially shaded site. Propagation is by seed when ripe, or spring, or cuttings from summer to autumn.

J. angulare (Zone 9) (*J. capense*) (S Africa) gained the RHS Award of Merit in 1956, but is seldom seen in Britain though it makes a fine frost-free greenhouse plant for a late summer display. A scrambling to semi-twining plant, it has glossy, evergreen leaves of three, rarely five, ovate leaflets to 4 cm long. The sweetly scented white flowers are borne in terminal clusters, each with a slender tube to about 4 cm long and five to seven (usually six) narrowly ovate lobes with rolled margins.

J. azoricum (Zone 9) (*J. trifoliatum*) (Madeira) does not, as its name suggests, come from the Azores but appears to be endemic to Madeira. It is extraordinarily like *J. angulare* and the two are con-fused in cultivation. This species has lanceolate petal lobes only 3-4 mm wide; those of *angulare* are 5-7 mm. The flowers are flushed purple in bud, whereas in *angulare* they may or may not be tinted pink.

J

J. beesianum (Zone 6) (China) is a deciduous, bushy semi-twiner, especially in open sunny sites. In shade it can climb to 2 m or more. The leaves are simple, ovate to lanceolate, 3-5 cm long and deep green. The flowers are velvety carmine about 1.5 cm wide but with rolled petals and appearing smaller. They are said to be fragrant, but I have been unable to detect any fragrance. Glossy black fruits follow which, when in sufficient numbers, make the plant quite conspicuous. This is an interesting little climber, but really rather short of beauty. See also *J.* X *stephanense*.

J. dispermum (Zone 8-9) (Himalayas to south western China) is a deciduous species to several metres in height and is rather like *J. officinale* in garden impact. It needs a very sheltered wall or frost-free greenhouse in Britain.

J. floridum (Zone 8) (Central China) has a loose shrubby to scrambling habit and evergreen leaves mainly trifoliate, but sometimes with five leaflets. The yellow, 2 cm long flowers open in late summer and autumn. In Britain, this species needs a warm sheltered wall.

J. lineare (Zone 9) (*J. lineatum*) (Australia) has very distinctive foliage, the leaves being simple, very narrow, 2-5 cm long and deep green. The white flowers are usually pink to a light reddish-purple-flushed in bud and very sweetly scented. Each one is about 1.5-2 cm wide with six to eight narrow petal lobes. This species is sometimes considered to be the climbing phase of the shrubby *J. suavissimum*. In Britain it needs a frost-free greenhouse.

J. mesnyi (Zone 8) (*J. primulinum*) (primrose jasmine) much resembles an evergreen *J. nudiflorum* (q.v.) with larger, six to ten-petalled flowers in spring and summer. It is best treated as a greenhouse plant in Britain though it does grow outside on warm walls unless the winter is severe.

J. nitidum (Zone 9) (angel wing, windmill or star jasmine) (Admiralty Islands, Southern Pacific) requires cool greenhouse conditions in Britain. It is a semi-climber to 3 m with simple, glossy leaves, elliptic-lanceolate in outline and up to 7 cm long. The fragrant, purplish-red-budded white flowers are 2.5-3.5 cm in width with up to ten or more narrow petal lobes.

J. nudiflorum (Zone 5) (winter jasmine) (China) hardly qualifies as a climber being no more than a weak scrambler at the most. It is, nevertheless, well worth tying to a wall or old standing tree trunk for the sake of its cheering winter blooms. Once established it should be thinned out annually after flowering to maintain plenty of young flowering stems. Trained like this it can reach 4 m or more. The stems are green for the first full year and bear pairs of trifoliate, rich glossy green leaves. From late autumn to early spring they are garlanded with bright yellow 2-2.5 cm wide and long flowers with six petal lobes. This highly garden-worthy plant was introduced by Robert Fortune in 1844 and has been popular ever since. It was given the RHS Award of Merit in 1923.

J. officinale (Zone 7-8) (common jasmine) has a wide range in the wild, from the Caucasus and northern Iran along the Himalayas and into China. It has graced British gardens for more than 400 years and has long been *the* white-flowered jasmine extolled by authors of all kinds. It is a vigorous climber capable of reaching 10 m in height, but is usually less. The pinnate leaves are composed of five to seven leaflets (rarely nine), the largest terminal one being up to 6 cm long, taper-pointed and sometimes with a deep notch on one side. The summer-borne, sweetly scented flowers are 2-2.5 cm long carried in terminal clusters on lateral leafy shoots. Glossy black fruits follow, but usually rather sparingly. *J. o.* 'Affine' has somewhat larger flowers, pink tinted in bud. *J. o.* 'Aureum' presents the appearance of having been flicked at with a brushful of yellow paint, such is the irregularity of its variegation. It is certainly a striking plant, but for me at least, not very pleasing.

J. polyanthum (Zone 9) (China) was discovered by Père Jean Marie Delavay in 1883 and George Forrest found it in 1906. Later, in 1931, Lawrence Johnston collected it and grew it in the south of France and gave a plant to fellow Riviera gardener Captain de la Warre. It was material from the Captain's garden that was featured in *The Botanical Magazine* of 1938. Finally, and at long last, gardeners became aware of this fine plant and an accolade of an Award of Merit in 1941 and a First Class Certificate in 1949 were given by the RHS. In effect, this is a highly floriferous, more strongly scented and pink budded version of *J. officinale*. Regrettably it is less hardy but makes a superb plant for a frost-free greenhouse. There it flowers in spring and early summer. Given more winter warmth (6°-7°C minimum) it will start to flower in late winter.

J. primulinum, see *J. mesnyi*.

J. X *stephanense* (Zone 7-8) (*J. beesianum* X *officinale*) is known to occur in the wild, but was purposefully created in France by Thomas Javitt before 1920 and taken up by the nursery firm of Lemoine and Son of Nancy. It favours *officinale* in general appearance, but among the pinnate leaves are simple ones and the flowers are light pink. At least some of the leaves are usually more or less creamy-white mottled, a genetic legacy of its hybrid origin and not especially decorative.

J. suavissimum, see *J. lineare*.

J. subhumile (Zone 8) (eastern Himalayas) has been known as *J. diversifolium* and *J. heterophyllum*. It can behave as a tall, loose shrub or small tree but also pushes through adjacent plants like a scrambler. With its glossy, thick-textured, deciduous leaves, which

101

are mainly ovate and simple, but sometimes trifoliate, it makes a distinctive wall cover, especially when spangled by its small, starry yellow flowers in late spring or early summer.

Kadsura *Schisandraceae*

The 22 species in this E Asian and W Malaysian genus are twining evergreens closely allied to *Schisandra*. Most species are tender, but one, *K. japonica* (Zone 8) will thrive outside in sheltered sites in Britain. This species is native to China, Japan and Taiwan and in cultivation can exceed 3 m in height. The slender stems bear oval to lance-shaped, taper pointed, glossy deep green leaves 5-10 cm long. From mid-summer to autumn solitary cream to pale yellow flowers open successively from the upper leaf axils. Each flower is about 2 cm wide and composed of six to nine rather fleshy textured petals. It is followed by a fruit resembling a spherical, 2-3 cm wide cluster of scarlet berries. *K. j.* 'Variegata' has cream-bordered leaves. This is a modest climber but of unusual appearance. Regrettably it is now difficult to obtain from a commercial source. Culture is as for *Schisandra*, but neutral to acid soil is also necessary.

Kennedia (Coral pea) *Leguminosae*

All of the 15 species in this genus are from Australia. All are evergreen trailers or twiners with pea-shaped flowers somewhat like those of *Clianthus*, but smaller and less pointed. They grow in ordinary well-drained soil, preferably neutral to acid. In Britain, the species mentioned below need a frost-free greenhouse but can be tried in very sheltered warm corners outside. Propagation is by seeds and cuttings in spring.

K. coccinea (Zone 9) is the coral pea of W Australia, a climber to 2 m or more that also can be used as a trailer. It has leaves mainly composed of three, but sometimes five, ovate leaflets, each to 5 cm long. When young they are silky hairy. In spring and early summer, long-stalked umbels of 1-1.5 cm long scarlet flowers expand. Each umbel has three to twelve flowers, and a well-flowered plant provides an eye-catching sight.

K. nigricans (Zone 9) (black coral pea) (W Australia) climbs to 3 m or more and in spring produces one-sided racemes of sombre, but intriguing, flowers of dark chocolate-purple and yellow. The foliage is dark and glossy, some leaves trifoliate, others entire, broadly ovate-cordate.

K. rubicunda (Zone 9) (dusky coral pea) has a wide range in Australia except the western part. It grows to about 3 m tall with slender stems covered in brown, downy hairs. The leaves are trifoliate, each leaflet broadly ovate, 5-10 cm and deep green. Dusky-red, 3-4 cm long flowers open in short axillary racemes from spring to mid-summer.

Lagenaria (bottle gourd) *Cucurbitaceae*

Although six species of tendril climbers or trailers are known in this genus, only one, *L. siceraria* (Zone 9-10) is widely grown. On archaeological evidence it appears to be one of the most ancient crops cultivated by man in the tropics. It resembles *Cucurbita* in essential details and cultural requirements, but the flowers are five-petalled, white and open out flat. *L. siceraria* probably arose in Africa but had reached tropical America long before Columbus. It is likely that the fruits, which are known to survive immersion in sea water for at least six months, drifted across from Africa in the Benguela current. It is a fast-growing annual plant capable, at least in warm countries, of growing 10 m or more in its one growing season. The long-stalked leaves are broadly ovate to rounded with a cordate base, up to 30 cm wide, and softly white-hairy beneath. In some forms the leaves are three to seven-lobed. The white flowers are up to 10 cm wide, sometimes more, and though showy, last for less than a day. They are followed by hard-rinded fruits of enormously varied shapes and sizes formerly much used by tropical peoples as domestic utensils, including bottles, bowls and ladles and as fishing-net floats and musical instruments.

Lapageria (Chilean bellflower) *Philesiaceae* (*Liliaceae*)

One unique species comprises this Chilean genus. *L. rosea* (Zone 8-9) is Chile's national flower and there known as copihue. It is a twining evergreen growing to 5 m with alternate, leathery-textured, semi-glossy, deep green ovate leaves up to 10 cm or more in length. During summer and autumn a succession of elegantly shaped pendent bell flowers opens from the leaf axils. Each waxy-textured bloom is about 7.5 cm long and, in the typical form, crimson with somewhat lighter freckling. The edible yellowish green, oblong fleshy fruits are technically berries, the sticky pulp containing several ovoid seeds. The latter, providing they are not allowed to dry out, provide a ready but slow means of increase. At about 10°-13°C the seeds take five weeks to germinate and three to five years must then elapse before flowers appear. The best compost is one largely composed of leaf mould and peat, though any freely drained neutral to acid soil is satisfactory. In Britain, copihue needs a frost-free greenhouse or a very sheltered site outside. It enjoys summer warmth, but prefers a partially shaded site. In its native country it garlands the trees and shrubs of thickets and woods, in a few places right by the road. When in full bloom it presents a wayside spectacle hard to beat anywhere. Several cultivars are known in Chile and some of these are occasionally grown in the northern hemisphere. Some are larger, paler, or striped, others white or almost so. In Britain 'Nash Court'

L

and 'Albiflora' are sometimes available. The first mentioned is soft, rich pink; the latter white with a faint hint of rose.

Lardizabala *Lardizabalaceae*

The two species of evergreen twiners which form this genus are confined to Chile. They have similar cultural preferences to that of *Lapageria* and are seldom seen. *L. biternata* (Zone 9) has been commercially available in the recent past. It is a vigorous species to 4 m or so with compound leaves composed of three to nine leathery-textured glossy ovate leaflets 5-10 cm long. The flowers are unisexual, the males 2 cm wide in pendent spikes 7-10 cm long. Individual flowers have six, fleshy, chocolate-purple sepals, the tiny petals modified to nectaries. The female flowers are larger and solitary and are followed by 5-7.5 cm long, sausage-shaped, dark purple edible fruits.

Lathyrus (everlasting and sweet pea) *Leguminosae*

Depending on the botanical authority there are 100 to 150 species in this genus of annuals and perennials. Not all are climbers but most of those that do, have leaves composed of two leaflets and a branched tendril. The flowers are carried in racemes from the upper leaf axils and are typically pea-like with a large, rounded, erect back or standard petal. Any fertile soil is suitable, the annual *L. odoratus* thriving best of all in a humus-rich medium. A sunny site is best. Propagation is by seed when ripe or in spring; the perennial species may also be propagated by division, or basal cuttings. In Britain, sweet peas are often sown in autumn in a cold frame or *in situ* under cloches. A better germination can be expected if the seeds are first soaked for 24 hours. When the seedlings have three true leaves, the tip is pinched out to promote strong basal shoots. This treatment produces bigger and earlier flowering plants.

L. latifolius (Zone 5) (everlasting pea) (Europe, widely naturalised in USA) is a perennial clump-former, sending up stems to 3 m or so annually. The leaflets are ovate to lanceolate 4-10 cm long. In late summer five to fifteen flowered racemes appear, individual blossoms being rose-purple or pure white and 2-3 cm wide. This is a long-lived and reliable species, very tolerant as to soil and even performing well on sand dunes when naturalised there as it is in Norfolk and elsewhere.

L. magellanicus (Zone 8-9) (Lord Anson's pea) is the famous everlasting blue pea from the Straits of Magellan in S America. It is akin to *L. pubescens* (q.v.) but has purple-blue flowers.

L. odoratus (Zone 3) (Southern Italy and Sicily) is the highly familiar sweet pea, a florist's flower *par excellence* and the subject of specialist societies. An annual climber to 2 m or more it has greyish-green ovate to elliptic leaflets and 2-3 cm wide fragrant flowers with a purplish-crimson standard and bright purple wing petals. Self-coloured forms were raised before the 1850s. In 1870, Henry Eckford began to breed new kinds purposefully, and other nursery-men/plant breeders followed. Eckford was, however, the most successful, gaining 31 awards between 1870 and 1900. The nursery firm of Unwin also came to the fore. In 1900 the cultivars 'Countess Spencer' and 'Gladys Unwin' were raised. Both were in shades of pale pink, the former being larger. Both had large, waved standard petals and were derived from an earlier pink sort, 'Prima Donna'. They mark the era of the modern sweet pea, sometimes still known as 'Spencer' varieties though ironically it was 'Gladys Unwin' that bred true and was the primary parent of the new race. Nowadays there are hundreds of cultivars with waved, self, bicoloured and picotee blooms to 4.5 cm diameter in practically every colour of the rainbow. There are also dwarf and semi-dwarf races. All the named cultivars are the result of painstaking breeding. The choice of what to grow depends on the colours and heights one requires, and a good specialist seedsman's catalogue is needed; Bolton's of Birdbrook, Essex, can be recommended.

L. pubescens (Zone 8-9) (Chile and Uruguay) superficially resembles *latifolius* but is downy-hairy and has more than two leaf-lets per leaf and usually ten or more flowers to each raceme. The latter are also larger and a delightful shade of lavender-blue. It needs a sheltered site in Britain and makes an attractive large pot plant for a frost-free greenhouse.

L. rotundifolius (Zone 6) (Persian everlasting pea) is native to western Asia, Crimea to central USSR. It is a slender perennial 80-100 cm tall, with rounded leaflets 3-6 cm long. Racemes of three to eight rose-coloured 2 cm wide flowers open in summer. This is the smallest and most graceful of the everlasting peas and looks charming covering up the bare base of a wall shrub.

Littonia *Liliaceae*

This genus contains six to eight tuberous rooted perennials from Africa, only one of which, *L. modesta* (Zone 9) is much cultivated. In general appearance this is almost identical to a small (about 1 m tall) *Gloriosa* (q.v.) but with nodding, 4 cm wide bowl-shaped flowers formed of six bright orange tepals. Cultivation as for *Gloriosa*. In Britain it is best in a greenhouse, making an unusual and appealing pot plant.

Lonicera (honeysuckle) *Caprifoliaceae*

About 200 species of shrubs and climbers form this northern hemis-phere genus. The climbers, some of which are evergreen, the rest

105

deciduous, are twiners with opposite pairs of usually simple leaves and terminal clusters of tubular flowers. The latter are borne in pairs, each one divided at the mouth into two lips, the broad upper one formed of four fused petal lobes, the lower a single lobe. In the majority of the climbing species cultivated, the flower clusters terminate short side shoots, the upper one or two pairs of leaves being connate, that is fused around the stem to form a disc or shallow bowl. Ordinary fertile soil and a site sheltered from the strongest winds are the main cultural requirements. The tender species need a greenhouse or a very warm corner outside. Propagation is by seeds when ripe or cuttings in summer or autumn.

L. alseuosmoides (Zone 5) (China) forms a splendid rich, evergreen cover of lush foliage, with its willow-like 3-5 cm long leaves. The 1.2-1.5 cm long flowers are too small to be showy, but well worth a close look. They are yellow without and purple within, almost equally five-lobed at the mouth and carried in leafy panicles from late summer to autumn. The twinned berries are small and black with a purplish waxy patina.

L. X *americana* (Zone 5) (*L. caprifolium* X *etrusca*) nicely blends the characters of its parents but with a rather larger nod towards *caprifolium*. It is very vigorous and capable of well exceeding 10 m given the opportunity. The young stems are violet-purple and the leaves are a rich, somewhat glossy green above, glaucous beneath. On non-flowering stems they are broadly elliptic, to 7 cm long. On the shorter flowering stems they are smaller and obovate. Depending on the vigour of the stems, the last one to three pairs below the flower clusters are connate, the broadest pair being immediately below the flower stalk. The 4-5 cm long, strongly two-lipped, fragrant flowers are red-purple in bud, opening white and ageing yellowish. They are carried in one or two closely set whorls on a 3-6 cm stalk above the topmost pair of connate leaves. On young or really vigorous plants three stalks may arise from this upper connate leaf pair, the centre, strongest one with its own smaller connate leaves. Occasionally there are further branches and a leafy panicle is built up. Quite often there is a fused pair of leafy bracts immediately beneath the flower cluster. I have described this very fine honeysuckle in some detail because it is the subject of considerable confusion in gardens. For a start there are at least two forms, one less vigorous and with paler red-purple buds. The more richly coloured of the two is frequently seen in cottage and suburban gardens where it parades as the 'Belgica' or 'Serotina' cultivars of the common honeysuckle, *L. periclymenum*. At least some nurserymen are guilty of this error. Superficially, these two entities are alike, but *periclymenum* does not have connate leaves so is easily separated from X *americana*. The latter also blooms much earlier; on a warm wall flowers start to open in late April, with the main display in May and early June.

L. X *brownii* (Zone 6-7) (*L. sempervirens* X *hirsuta*) much resembles the first parent and is sometimes confused with it. However, whereas *sempervirens* has an almost regularly five-lobed mouth to the flower, X *brownii* has a shortly two-lipped one. The flower tube is also glandular-hairy, not smooth as in *sempervirens*, and the connate leaves below the flowers are oval, not almost rounded. *L.* X *b.* 'Fuchsioides' is almost identical, perhaps marginally finer. 'Plantierensis' is even more like *sempervirens* but the flowers still show the *hirsuta* hairs. 'Dropmore Scarlet', raised more recently (Gold Medal at the Boskoop Trials in 1964), is said to be superior and with a longer flowering season.

L. caprifolium (Zone 5) (Europe, western Asia) has been considered a British native also, but is now known to be naturalised in its few widely scattered localities. Climbing to 8 m or so in height, it has ovate to oblong leaves 4-7 cm or more long, dark green above, glaucous beneath. The upper two to three pairs on the flowering stems are connate, the uppermost being the broadest and in the centre of which sits a stalkless flower cluster. The 4-5 cm long flowers are white to deep cream, sometimes pink-tinted in bud. *L. c.* 'Pauciflora' has more deeply suffused flower buds.

L. etrusca (Zone 7) (Mediterranean region) can be semi-evergreen to deciduous, depending on the severity of the winter. It can reach 10 m in height but is usually less in Britain. The 4-9 cm long leaves are oval to obovate, glaucous and more or less downy beneath. The upper one to three pairs below the flowers are connate. Fragrant, cream ageing yellow, 4 cm long flowers open in stalked clusters above the upper united leaf pair, in late summer. Quite often the flower buds are red suffused. In Britain it is not as satisfactory a performer outside as is its hybrid *L.* X *americana*.

L. flava (Zone 5) has a very local distribution in its native south eastern USA and is rarely seen in cultivation, at least in Britain. A fairly robust climber to about 5 m, it has almost round leaves 6-9 cm long and greyish beneath. The upper leaves on the flowering stems are connate, the topmost pair being very large and bowl-shaped. Within this bowl sits a stalkless cluster of broad-petalled, yellow flowers which age to reddish-orange. Each cluster comprises 15 to 20 flowers and the overall effect is both showy and highly distinctive. Owing to the kindness of Mrs Pamela Harper of Virginia, USA, I now grow this neglected species in my Norfolk garden and look forward to making it better known. Unfortunately, it is not so easy to propagate as most honeysuckles.

L. X *heckrottii* (Zone 5) 'Gold Flame' has an unrecorded history but was first noticed in the USA in 1895 and named by the botanist

107

Alfred Rehder. He considered its parentage to be *L.* X *americana* X *sempervirens* and nobody has since disputed this calculated guess. At its best it is more of a scrambler than a true climber, to about 4 m, rather curious considering that its putative parents are good twiners, at least when young. In general appearance it resembles a superior X *americana* with panicle-like clusters of yellow, red-budded flowers.

L. henryi (Zone 5) (China) much resembles *L. alseuosmoides* but has hairy stems and larger, relatively broader leaves 5-10 cm long. The 2 cm long yellow, purple-red-suffused flowers are borne in terminal clusters around mid-summer.

L. hildebrandiana (Zone 9) (Burma, Cambodia, China) is the giant of its genus, reaching up into trees for 20-25 m. Its evergreen, oval leaves are 7-15 cm long, rich green above, paler beneath. The paired fragrant flowers arise in leaf axils and in terminal racemes from mid to late summer. Each slender bloom is 12-18 cm long, opening to almost white and soon ageing to soft brownish-orange. In most of Britain this species needs a frost-free to cool greenhouse but few amateur greenhouses are large enough, especially as it does not flower well until of a good size.

L. implexa (Zone 7) (Minorca honeysuckle) is closely allied to *L. etrusca* and has a similar Mediterranean range in the wild. In Britain it rarely grows to more than 3 m and is slower growing than most honeysuckles.

L. japonica (Zone 6-8) (Japan, Korea, China) varies considerably in hardiness, vigour and leaf shape. Basically it is a fast-growing evergreen twiner to 10 cm with 3-8 cm long oval to elliptic leaves carried on densely hairy stems. The fragrant flowers are 2.5-3.5 cm long, white ageing yellow, in axillary pairs from mid-summer to autumn. It is exuberantly naturalised in parts of eastern USA where it is considered a pest. The following three entities mainly represent it in gardens. *L. j.* 'Aureoreticulata' has small, broad leaves, sometimes lobed, the vein pattern picked out in yellow. Unlike most variegated plants it is as hardy as the type. 'Halliana' is very close to the type, with bright green leaves and highly fragrant flowers. It needs a sheltered site in Britain and was killed in my garden during the 1981-2 winter when the temperature twice dropped to $-13°$C. 'Repens' (*L. j. repens*) is similar to 'Halliana' but is less strong-growing; the shoots, leaves and flowers are flushed purple.

L. periclymenum (Zone 4) (Europe, W Asia, N Africa) is the common honeysuckle or woodbine and the only climbing species native to Britain. Given the opportunity it can climb to at least 6 m but is usually much less. The 3-7 cm long leaves may be ovate, elliptic or oblong, fairly rich green above, glaucous beneath. Leaves and stems may be smooth or hairy. Strong vigorous shoots may bear lobed leaves. From mid-summer to autumn a succession of 4-5 cm long fragrant flowers are carried in terminal clusters. Basically they open creamy-white and age to a yellowish shade. Some plants regularly produce flowers tinted or flushed purple in the bud. *L. p.* 'Belgica' is the so-called early Dutch honeysuckle with the flower buds richly flushed purple-red. In Britain, at least, it appears to have been partially supplanted by *L.* X *americana* (q.v.). *L. p.* 'Serotina' ('Late Red') goes under the name of late Dutch, reputedly flowering from late summer (July) onwards. It appears to be confused with 'Belgica' and X *americana*. There is a plant listed as 'Serotina Winchester' which I have not seen. A coloured photograph, however, shows a typical X *americana* or possibly X *heckrottii*.

L. sempervirens (Zone 7 to Zone 4 in USA) (trumpet honey-suckle) (eastern USA) varies from evergreen to deciduous, depending on the severity of the winter. It is the most distinctive in bloom of all the climbing honeysuckles, with slenderly tubular flowers to 5 cm long, the mouth divided into five short, equal lobes. They are not fragrant but wonderfully showy, deep orange-scarlet, paler within the mouth. There is a rare cultivar, 'Sulphurea', with clear, soft yellow flowers. The plant can reach 8 m in height and has oval to obovate leaves 4-6 cm in length, rich, almost glossy green above, glaucous beneath. The upper leaves on the flowering stems are connate, the topmost pair almost circular and saucer-shaped, above which the flowers are carried in spikes of three to six well-spaced whorls from mid-summer to autumn. It was once considered to be a greenhouse plant in Britain, perhaps because it was originally grown from material gathered in the extreme south of its natural range (Florida, Georgia). On a sheltered, sunny wall it should grow well in most parts.

L. X *tellmanniana* (Zone 6) (*L. tragophylla* X *sempervirens*) was raised at the Royal Hungarian Horticultural School, Budapest, was put into commerce in Germany by the nurseryman Späth in 1927 and soon reached Britain where it gained an RHS Award of Merit in 1931. A deciduous plant growing to at least 6 m, it strongly favours the *tragophylla* parent, exclusively as to flower shape. The flowers are, however, only 5 cm long, bright yellow flushed coppery-orange and red. It is one of the few honeysuckles which will flower well in shade.

L. tragophylla (Zone 6) (China) was discovered by Augustine Henry and later introduced by E.H. Wilson in 1900. Next to *hildebrandiana* it is one of the largest in leaf and flower. The latter are up to 9 cm long, bright yellow, in clusters of ten to twenty above a pair of connate leaves, in summer. The lower, stalked leaves are 6-12 cm long, and slightly blue-grey tinted on both surfaces. The RHS conferred an Award of Merit in 1913 and the AGM in 1928. This is a highly distinctive and beautiful species, all the more valuable because it needs a really shaded site to thrive.

Figure 5.14
Mandevilla laxa

I. INCH   1·2·49

M

Mandevilla *Apocynaceae*

Although more than a hundred species are credited to this tropical S American genus, only a few are widely cultivated. They are twiners, with opposite pairs of leaves and terminal clusters of trumpet-shaped flowers, which are of very handsome appearance in some species. Slender twinned seed pods follow. Except *M. laxa*, the species described need a cool greenhouse in Britain, making attractive pot plants. Ordinary soil or a proprietary compost are suitable. Propagation is by seeds in spring or cuttings of firm stem sections in summer, both at 18°-21°C.

M. boliviensis (Zone 9) (*Dipladenia boliviensis*) is native to both Bolivia and Ecuador, climbing to 4 m or more in height. It has rich, lustrous green narrowly oblong leaves to about 10 cm long. In summer, clusters of three to seven orange-yellow-eyed white flowers open in succession, each one about 5 cm wide.

M. laxa (Zone 8) (*M. suaveolens*) is sometimes known as Chilean jasmine though it comes from Argentina, Bolivia and Peru. It is a deciduous twiner to at least 5 m with slender-pointed, heart-shaped based, oblong to ovate leaves 5-10 cm in length. From about mid-summer to early autumn, small clusters of fragrant white flowers like a giant jasmine open in succession. Each fragrant flower is about

5 cm long, narrowly funnel-shaped, with five wide spreading, angular lobes. In Britain a warm sheltered wall is essential and in the colder areas a frost-free greenhouse gives the best results.

M. sanderi (Zone 9-10) (Brazil) climbs to 5 m or so, with leathery glossy, 4-5 cm long ovate-oblong leaves. The rose-pink, yellow-eyed flowers are up to 7.5 cm wide and extremely decorative. They open mainly in summer, but providing the temperature is above about 15°C they can be seen at almost any time of the year.

M. splendens (Zone 9-10) (*Dipladenia splendens*) is a native of Brazil and can be seen in forests on the Organ Mountains near Rio de Janeiro. In cultivation it grows to about 3 m, the slender stems clad with lustrous, elliptic leaves 12-20 cm long. The flowers are the largest of the species cultivated, being at least 10 cm and sometimes up to 13 cm wide. It is mainly represented by *D. s. profusa* with rich carmine flowers and *D. s. williamsii* having pink blooms with a carmine throat. This is a tuberous-rooted species and is best cut back to near ground level each late winter and kept on the dry side until growth starts again.

Manettia *Rubiaceae*

More than 100 species names are listed under this mainly tropical American genus but only one is widely cultivated. *M. inflata* (Zone 9) (*M. bicolor*) comes from Paraguay and Uruguay but is sometimes known as Brazilian firecracker vine. It is a soft-stemmed evergreen perennial twiner growing to 1.2 m in height with pairs of lustrous, rich green ovate leaves to 7 cm long. The long-stalked tubular flowers arise in the upper leaf axils from spring to autumn. Each one is about 1.8 cm long, covered with short thick hairs and rather like towelling in texture, scarlet with a yellow mouth and five short petal lobes. Ordinary soil or compost is suitable, with minimum winter temperature of 5°C. In Britain a greenhouse is necessary. Propagation is by cuttings in summer. The plant grown formerly under the name of *bicolor* has narrow calyx lobes; *inflata* has broad, almost leafy ones, but this character is variable and the two are now united.

Maurandya, see *Asarina*.

Menispermum (Moonseed) *Menispermaceae*

The two species in this genus are widely separated geographically, one in eastern North America, the other in NE Asia. They are closely related to *Cocculus* (q.v.) and basically resemble it, but the small flowers have four to ten sepals and six to nine petals. *Cocculus* consistently has six of each. Culture as for *Cocculus*.

M. canadense (Zone 4) (yellow parilla) twines up to 4 m, with handsome, rounded, entire or shallowly lobed leaves up to 20 cm

111

long, the stalk appearing to come from underneath (peltate). Small whitish or greenish flowers arise in axillary racemes in summer and are followed by small black, berry-like fruits with a white waxy patina. The single seed in each fruit is flattened and crescent-shaped, hence the name moonseed. From a garden point of view the Asiatic *M. dauricum* is identical. Botanically it is distinguished by having two racemes of flowers from each leaf axil (*canadense* has only one).

Mikania *Compositae*

Depending upon the botanical authority there are 150-250 species in this mainly tropical American genus. One evergreen twining species is fairly widely grown, *M. scandens* (Zone 9) from south eastern USA, and widely naturalised in warm countries elsewhere. Known also as climbing hempweed, it grows 2-5 m in height with pairs of triangular to heart-shaped, long-pointed glossy leaves to 10 cm long. In autumn, the upper leaf axils produce stalked clusters of fluffy groundsel-like flower heads which may be white or flesh coloured. It thrives best in moisture retentive soil in sun or partial shade. In Britain it needs a very sheltered site or a frost-free greenhouse. Propagation is by cuttings from spring to autumn.

Mina *Convolvulaceae*

One species, *M. lobata* from Mexico to S America, comprises this genus. It is very closely related to *Ipomoea* and has been included in that genus by some botanists. The flowers are narrowly tubular and slightly curved, each with protruding stamens. They start scarlet and gradually age to orange and yellow and are carried in forked racemes from the upper leaf axils. The leaves are deeply three-lobed with the suggestion of an extra lobe on either side. They are about 7 cm wide and make a pleasing foil for the flowers. Well-grown plants can attain 4 m or more but are much less when grown as an annual. In warm climates it is a short-lived perennial. The general culture and propagation is as for *Ipomoea*.

Momordica (balsam apple) *Cucurbitaceae*

The 40 species in this tropical African and Asian genus are fast growing tendril clingers. Some species, including those described below, are grown for their edible immature and ornamental mature fruits. These are gourd-like, but unlike the true gourds they split open into three irregular segments to disclose the orange or red aril-covered seeds. As in other members of the gourd family, the flowers are unisexual and are carried in the leaf axils. The rounded leaves are deeply lobed. In Britain, at least, the annual species dealt with below are best in a cool or cold greenhouse and make a decorative tapestry trained on the back wall of a lean-to. In warm, sheltered corners it can be grown outside. Ordinary fertile soil is suitable. Propagation is by seeds sown in spring at 18°-21°C, ideally singly in small pots.

M. balsamina (Zone 9) (balsam apple) (Africa, Asia, Australia) is an annual growing to 4 m or so with 10-15 cm wide, sharply lobed leaves and 7 cm wide yellow flowers. The fruits are ovoid to ellipsoid to 8 cm long, heavily warted, pale orange-yellow, containing orange-red seeds.

M. charantia (Zone 9) (bitter gourd, balsam pear) probably came from Africa, but is now extensively naturalised in the tropics. It resembles *M. balsamina* but the leaves have deeper blunt-tipped lobes and the fruits are longer, to 20 cm or more. In India and Asia the young bitter fruits are used in curries and as a vegetable, the bitterness being reduced by steeping the peeled fruits in salt water before cooking. The seed mass of the ripe fruits is used, in India at least, as a condiment and the shoot tips and young leaves are cooked in the same way as spinach. The bitter gourd is also used in native medicines.

Muehlenbeckia *Polygonaceae*

Most of the 15-20 species in this genus come from the warmer parts of Australasia, western S America and New Guinea. Only one New Zealand species is reasonably hardy.

M. complexa (Zone 7) is a twiner growing to 5 m with black-purple wiry stems and small, rounded, often lobed dark green leaves, usually with brownish-purple margins. The tiny, greenish flowers have five tepal lobes which, after flowering, swell up and become white and fleshy, partly surrounding the triangular, black nutlet in the centre. Regrettably this species is dioecious and as one rarely needs more than one plant, fruits are seldom seen. Grown without support *M. complexa* forms a complex (hence its name) rounded mass of intertwining stems rather like a sprawling low shrub. Ordinary soil in sun or shade is suitable. Propagation by cuttings in late summer.

Mutisia *Compositae*

This is one of the comparatively few genera of climbing plants in the daisy family. Its uniqueness is further added to by possessing leaf-tip tendrils; most of the others twine. *Mutisia* is restricted to S America and contains about 60 species of climbers, trailers and shrubs. Most sorts have simple, often stalkless, evergreen leaves and solitary, terminal flower heads composed of a cylindrical to cigar-shaped base of overlapping bracts (phyllaries) and up to ten or more ray petals. The climbing members are best grown over shrubs; in Britain the shelter of a wall is necessary or of a greenhouse in cold areas. Well

113

drained soil, preferably humus-rich and neutral to acid is the ideal though some species tolerate lime. Propagation is by seeds under glass in spring, cuttings in summer or removing suckers when possible in spring.

M. clematis (Zone 9) (Ecuador, Colombia, Peru) is one of the exceptions with pinnate leaves composed of five to nine oblong-oval leaflets. In the wild the plant can climb to 10 m but in cultivation it is seldom more than half this. The flower heads are nodding, 6-7 cm wide and a bright orange-scarlet. This is the showiest of the half-hardy mutisias flowering from early summer to autumn, but it is difficult to propagate and all too seldom seen.

M. decurrens (Zone 8) (Chile, Argentina) grows to 3 m in favourable sites with lance-shaped to narrowly oblong leaves 7-13 cm long. The 10 cm wide flowers are orange to orange-red and open during the summer. Apart from being showy, the flowers of this species have the greatest elegance, each of the 16 ray florets arching upwards and outwards in very neat formation. It is one of the hardiest species.

M. ilicifolia (Zone 9) (Chile) has leathery leaves to 6 cm long with holly-like spiny teeth. In some cases the 3-4 m long stems bear spiny-toothed wings or flanges. The 6-7.5 cm wide flowers vary from pink to pale mauve and open from spring to late summer. In a cool greenhouse it flowers almost continuously. It does not seem to appreciate coldish, wet winters but does stand drought well. I remember some ten years ago, when plant collecting in the foothills of the Andes, visiting an area that had just experienced several years of almost total drought. There among the rocks and dying scrub stunted plants of *Mutisia ilicifolia* still struggled on and even produced an odd bud or two.

M. oligodon (Zone 8) (Chile, Argentina) is, along with *M. decurrens*, one of the two hardiest species. It is very distinct in appearance, being only a partial climber and often functioning as a trailer. In the wild it forms suckering colonies of stems rarely above 30 cm tall, usually in dry, rocky places. The stems can be twice this length in cultivation, seldom more, and are clad with 2.5-4 cm long oblong, stalkless, leathery, spiny-toothed leaves that are white woolly beneath and glossy above. From summer to autumn they produce a succession of salmon-pink flower heads with six to twelve ray florets. Although described as long ago as 1835, it appears to have reached Britain only as a result of Harold F. Comber's 1925-7 expedition to the southern Andes. A plant at Borde Hill, raised from the original seed lived outside for over 40 years, giving some idea of its hardiness.

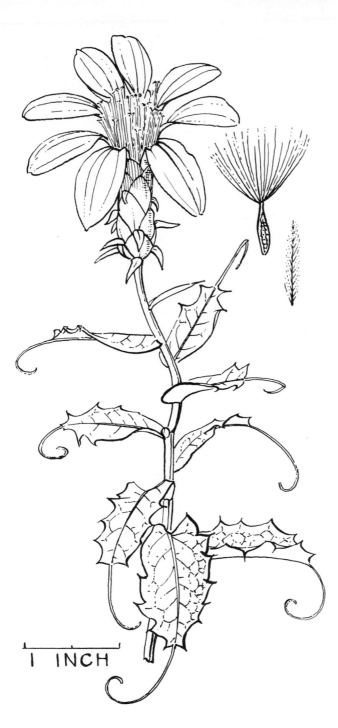

Figure 5.15
Mutisia oligodon

1 INCH

Figure 5.16
Mutisia decurrens

I INCH

O

Oxypetalum *Asclepiadaceae*

From among the estimated 125-150 species in this Mexican to South American genus, one only is widely grown. This is *O. caeruleum* (Zone 9) from Brazil to Uruguay, a plant with a chequered naming history, being at various times classified in two other genera, *Amblyopetalum* and *Tweedia*. It is a twining, woody-based perennial or sub-shrub, not usually above 1 m in height. It is downy-hairy with opposite pairs of 5-10 cm long, narrowly oblong to lance-shaped greyish-hazed leaves and axillary clusters of sky-blue flowers. The latter are five-petalled stars 2-5.3-5 cm wide and open from late summer to autumn. In Britain *O. caeruleum* is best as a summer annual outside or as a greenhouse perennial. It grows in ordinary soil in sun and is easily propagated by seeds or basal cuttings in spring.

Paederia *Rubiaceae*

Only one member of this Asian and American genus of about 50 species is likely to be seen in cultivation, at least in Britain. *P. scandens* (Zone 7) (*P. chinensis*) grows wild in China, Japan and Korea where it twines upwards for at least 6 m. It is deciduous with somewhat lustrous, dark green, ovate leaves 6-15 cm in length and makes a handsome wall cover, though beware the curiously foetid smell given off when the leaves are bruised. The 1 cm long, tubular flowers are whitish with purple eyes and are carried in panicles during late summer. They are followed by small, glossy orange berries. Any fertile soil in a sunny or partially shaded and sheltered site is suitable. Propagation is by cuttings in late summer.

Figure 5.17
*Pandorea
jasminoides*

1 INCH

Pandorea *Bignoniaceae*

At least two of the eight species in this genus of evergreen twiners from central Australia to Malaysia and New Guinea are widely cultivated. They have pinnate leaves in opposite pairs and axillary and

117

terminal panicles of tubular, somewhat foxglove-like flowers with five, spreading petal lobes. Ordinary, humus-rich soil and a sunny site are primary requirements. Under glass the plants are best confined to tubs; in a border they are apt to be very vigorous and flower less freely. Propagation is by cuttings in summer.

P. jasminoides (Zone 9) (bower vine, bower of beauty) (coast regions of Queensland and New South Wales, Australia) has been classified in both *Tecoma* and *Bignonia* in the past but now rests securely here. It is a slow growing climber to about 2 m or more, often behaving as a loose shrub. The leaves have five to nine dark green, glossy leaflets which beautifully enhance the 5-6 cm wide pink or white flowers, each with its startling eye of rich rose-crimson. Summer and autumn are the main flowering times.

P. pandorana (Zone 9-10) (wonga-wonga vine) (eastern Australia to New Guinea) gets its curious vernacular name from the Australian aborigines. It is a vigorous twiner to at least 6 m in height with pinnate, glossy leaves and axillary clusters of fragrant cream flowers with a crimson throat blotch. The individual flowers are smaller than those of *P. jasminoides*, but make up for this in their greater prodigality and fragrance. Their season too lasts for much of the year if it is warm enough, with the main flush in spring and early summer.

Parthenocissus (Virginia creeper) *Vitidaceae*

Temperate Asia and N America are the home countries of the 15 species of tendril climbers in this genus. They have broad, deciduous leaves which are either cut into three to seven separate leaflets or are broadly lobed. In most of the commonly grown sorts they colour richly before they fall. The tiny greenish, five-petalled flowers are insignificant but may be followed by small blue-black or blue grapes. Ordinary soil and sun or shade are adequate. Propagation is by late summer or late autumn cuttings, the latter inserted where they are to grow.

P. henryana (Zone 8) (*Vitis henryana*) (China) was discovered by Augustine Henry about 1885, but did not reach Britain until 1900 when E.H. Wilson, following up many of Henry's discoveries, collected seeds. It climbs to at least 8 m by the aid of sucker-tipped tendrils and has the most decorative foliage of all the cultivated species. Each leaf is composed of three to five obovate to oblanceolate leaflets about 5-10 cm long. They are a rich, almost velvety green with a silvery-white vein pattern often tinted pink. This variegation is best in partial to almost full shade and a well-grown plant on a north wall presents a most appealing sight. There is a bonus in autumn when the leaves turn red. Dark blue grapes are sometimes produced.

P. himalayana (Zone 8-9) (*Ampelopsis himalayana*) (Himalaya) is

118

regrettably not too hardy in Britain though it survives in sheltered places. It can attain 10 m in height and is a more or less efficient self-clinger. The 6-15 cm long trifoliate leaves are dark and glossy, turning crimson in autumn. Small blue fruits are sometimes produced. *P. semicordata* has smaller leaves, bristly hairy beneath, and is a little hardier.

P. inserta (Zone 2) (*Vitis inserta*) (N America) much resembles and is confused with the more familiar *P. quinquefolia* but is easily distinguished by the lack of suckers on the tendrils. It is a splendid plant for covering a big dead tree stump or even a living tree, especially when its cascading stems are covered with deep red autumn leaves.

P. quinquefolia (Zone 3) (*Vitis quinquefolia, V. hederacea*) is the true Virginian creeper of eastern USA (see also comments under *P. tricuspidata*). Known also in its native country as woodbine, this vigorous self-clinger can reach to at least 20 m when happily situated. It has digitate leaves composed of five, slender-tipped elliptic to obovate leaflets which are somewhat glaucous beneath (those of *P. inserta* are green and semi-glossy) and turn glowing crimson in autumn. The tiny bluish-black grapes are largely hidden by the leaves.

P. thomsonii (Zone 7) (*Vitis thomsonii*) (China to Himalayas) has as its nearest ally the better known *P. henryana*, but differs from it in its slightly smaller, red-purple flushed leaflets and lack of silvery veining. The young shoots are strongly suffused bright red-purple. In autumn the leaves change to bright shades of red. The fruits are black.

P. tricuspidata (Zone 4) (China, Japan, Korea) should, in Britain at least, be called Japanese creeper for it first reached these islands from Japan via the nurseryman and plant collector James G. Veitch in 1862. It proved to be one of the most successful of all climbing plants and is now ubiquitous on the walls of grand mansions and humble cottages throughout the land. Not only has it steadily supplanted the earlier introduced *P. quinquefolia*, but it has acquired its popular name also and added to the many horticultural confusions of naming. It has a similar success story in eastern USA and became so common in the Boston area that it acquired the name Boston ivy. A secure self-clinger, it can attain 20 m or more in height, the slender stems clad with somewhat lustrous, maple-like leaves with three pointed lobes. The intense crimson of the autumn leaves is one of the sights to be looked forward to in autumn. Rather hidden, the small grapes are dark blue with a waxy patina. It is a variable plant and has had over-much attention from the botanists. The following synonyms are still sometimes met with: *Ampelopsis tricuspidata, A. veitchii, Cissus veitchii, Vitis inconstans, Psedera tricuspidata*. The original collection is now designated *P. t.* 'Veitchii'. It has slightly smaller leaves, purple flushed when young. *P. t.* 'Lowii' is described as having small, three to seven-lobed leaves which are curiously crisped. The newer cultivar, 'Beverly Brook' appears to be similar but with flat leaves. The plant stocked under this name by Scotts Nurseries, Merriott, Somerset is like the line drawing of 'Lowii' in *Trees and Shrubs Hardy in the British Isles* (eighth ed.) Vol 3, p. 98. 'Beverly Brook' produces some trifoliate leaves and this has been noticed in some other forms, perhaps being a juvenile character.

Passiflora (passion flower) *Passifloraceae*

No less than 400 species are credited to this genus of woody and herbaceous climbers. Most species are native to the Americas, mainly southern, but a few occur in Asia and Australia. They are tendril clingers and, curiously enough, each tendril replaces a flower. The latter are unique in the plant world and missionaries to the 'New World' saw them as symbols of Christ's crucifixion and the subsequent conversion of the natives to Christianity. The base of each flower is tubular (in those species formerly classified as *Tacsonia* they are relatively long). At the top of the tube arise ten tepals which may spread out flat or overlap to form a bowl. From the centre arises a stalk bearing a ring of large anthers (the five wounds) and an ovoid to globular ovary surrounded by three large-knobbed styles (the three nails). This combined male and female organ is known as an androphore. Around its base and borne on top of the flower tube is a ring of filaments (the crown of thorns). In the former tacsonias these are very short but in some passifloras they are very long, e.g. *P. quadrangularis*. The flowers are usually pendent and open in summer and autumn. Humus-rich soil and partial to full sun are the ideal conditions. Under glass they are best confined to tubs. Propagation is by cuttings in summer or seeds in spring, both at 18°-21°C.

P. X *allardii* (Zone 9) (*P. caerulea* 'Constance Elliott' X *P. quadrangularis*) was raised at the University Botanic Garden, Cambridge by a former superintendent, Mr E.J. Allard. It resembles the first parent in a general way but is more robust, usually has three-lobed leaves and larger flowers.

P. antioquiensis (Zone 9) (*Tacsonia van-volxemii*) (Colombia) is akin to *mollissima* (q.v.) but has more narrowly lobed leaves and larger, showy, rose-red flowers. It makes a lovely climber for a frost-free greenhouse.

P. caerulea (Zone 8-9) (common or blue passion flower) is, despite its central and western S American homeland, surprisingly hardy in Britain. Though it often gets cut back to ground level in a cold winter it usually springs up again, either from the stem base or direct from the roots. It grows to 10 m or more and is capable of doing half of this in one season. The 10-15 cm wide leaves are deeply five to nine-fingered and dark green. The 6-10 cm wide flowers open out flat with white or pinkish tepals and a blue, white or purple-banded corona. The ovoid, pale orange-yellow fruits are 3-4 cm long. *P. c.* 'Constance Elliott' has entirely white flowers.

P. X *caeruleoracemosa* (Zone 9) (*P. caerulea* X *racemosa*) favours the latter of the two parent species with larger three-lobed leaves and purple flowers. 'Eynsford Gem' has soft mauve-pink flowers.

P. X *caponii* (Zone 9) (*P. quadrangularis* X *racemosa*) was raised at the John Innes Institute then at Bayfordbury, Hertford, Hertfordshire, by Mr W.J. Capon in 1953. Only one seedling germinated and as it looked like *P. quadrangularis* it was assumed to be an accidental natural self (though this is rare). Soon it produced widely three-lobed leaves and later, big, bowl-shaped flowers superior to its mother. Scientific investigation showed this hybrid to be a sterile triploid with two sets of *quadrangularis* chromosomes to the one of *racemosa*. For a full description and history of this plant see the RHS *Journal* for 1960, p. 184-6. The 11-12.5 cm wide flowers are white flushed claret-purple, with four zones of filaments, the longest 4.5 cm long, sideways-twisted and boldly banded purple and white from a crimson base.

P. coccinea (Zone 9) (Venezuela to Brazil) has simple ovate leaves on purple-hued stems to 8 m or more. The 7-10 cm wide flowers are scarlet and very showy. It deserves to be seen in British greenhouses more often. Nevertheless there is a superior species, *P. vitifolia* with larger, more richly-toned blooms which should be given priority. Neither appears to be commercially available in Britain.

P. edulis (Zone 9) (Brazil, N Argentina) is the true passion fruit and is also known as purple granadilla. Reaching to 7 m or more it has deeply three-lobed, 10 cm wide leaves and 5-7 cm wide flowers. The latter are green and white with a purple zoned corona. In the type the almost globular 4-6 cm long fruits are dull purple. *P. e. flavicarpa* has greenish-yellow fruits.

P. X *exoniensis* (Zone 9) (*P. antioquiensis* X *mollissima*) is much like its similar parents but more vigorous and free flowering. The 10-13 cm wide flowers are rose-pink. It has been distributed as *P. mixta quitensis*.

P. mollissima (Zone 9) (*Tacsonia mollissima*) (banana passion fruit) (Venezuela to Bolivia) runs up to at least 10 m in height given the opportunity. It is widely naturalised in frost-free countries and can be a beautiful nuisance. The leaves are softly downy, deeply three-lobed and up to 10 cm in length. Long-tubed, the pink flowers are 6.5-9 cm wide with a corona reduced to a purple warted band. The shortly cylindrical 6-11 cm long fruits are yellowish and downy and yield a pleasant, acid juice.

P. quadrangularis (Zone 9-10) (giant granadilla) probably arose in tropical America but the exact locality is unknown. The most robust of all the cultivated passion flowers, it has sharply four-angled or winged stems to 8 m or so and oval leaves to 20 cm long. Each fragrant, bowl-shaped flower is 7.5-11.5 cm wide with white, pink or light violet petals. The corona is formed of five ranks or zones, the outer ones wavy and purple-banded, to 6 cm long. Ovoid, yellow fruits of somewhat melon-like appearance, 20-30 cm long, follow the flowers but are not commonly borne on greenhouse specimens. They are not strongly flavoured but are widely used in warm countries for making cooling drinks, flavouring sherbets and ice creams and for jam. The flesh is used in fruit salads and the immature fruits can be boiled as a vegetable.

P. racemosa (Zone 9) (Brazil) can attain 10 m or more in height in warm countries but is much less under glass. The stems are slender and bear leathery, glossy leaves to 10 cm long, usually with three forward-pointing wavy lobes. Unlike the other passion flowers in cultivation, *racemosa*, as its name indicates, bears its 8-10 cm wide starry red flowers in terminal, almost leafless sprays (racemes). A well-flowered plant provides an elegantly colourful spectacle fit for the greenhouse of a queen.

P. umbilicata (Zone 8-9) (Bolivia to N Argentina) seems to be equally as hardy as *P. caerulea* and deserves to be much more widely grown in the sheltered parts of Britain and other zone 8 areas. Attaining at least 8 m in height it has slender, ribbed stems and deeply three-lobed bright green leaves up to 5 cm long. The 4-5 cm wide flowers are amethyst to violet, each one with two mauve-purple bracts at the base.

P. vitifolia, see under *P. coccinea*.

Periploca (silk vine) *Asclepiadaceae*

About 10 species of shrubs and twiners from Africa and Asia comprise this genus. The climbers have slender stems and opposite pairs of simple leaves. Small, five-petalled, rather starry flowers are carried in clusters and are followed by intriguing forked seed pods. Within these pods are many neatly packed seeds each with a tuft of long, silky hairs (to aid dispersal by wind), hence the vernacular name. The species described here thrive in ordinary soil but need sunny, sheltered sites. Propagation is by seeds under glass in spring or cuttings in summer. Division, if convenient, in spring is an easy method. The milky sap is poisonous.

P. graeca (Zone 7-8) (SE Europe, western Turkey) is the common silk vine, a deciduous twiner 6-10 m in height. The ovate leaves are 5-10 cm long and prominently veined. In late summer, 2-3 cm wide flowers expand, the petals downy and slightly sticky, brownish-purple within, greenish-yellow in bud. The seed pods are 8-13 cm long and joined at the tips. The seeds within bear tufts of hair to 3 cm in length.

P. laevigata (Zone 9) (*P. angustifolia*) (Canary Islands) only just qualifies as a climber for although the stem tips twine, the plant can behave as a free-standing shrub. Under glass it behaves more as a true climber attaining several metres in height. The leaves are elliptic, 2.5-5 cm long, the flowers about 12 mm wide, violet to brownish purple. The pods fork at a wide angle, often almost horizontally.

P. sepium (Zone 7) (China) is the Chinese silk vine, a deciduous species much like *P. graeca* but with narrower leaves and deep purple flowers. It is also hardier.

Petrea (purple wreath) *Verbenaceae*

Despite higher estimates, there appears to be a total of 27 species of shrubs and climbers in this tropical American and West Indian genus. Only one, *P. volubilis* (Zone 9-10) is widely grown and suitable for a cool greenhouse in Britain. It twines rapidly to 10 m or more, with rough-textured elliptic leaves 5-20 cm in length and terminal trusses of flowers from late winter to autumn, depending on temperature. Individual flowers are 2.5-3.5 cm wide, with five deep violet petals and an equal number of much longer, narrower lilac-blue sepals forming a star. The flowers are carried in simple racemes, but many racemes arise together and a plant in full bloom presents a spectacular and beautiful sight. A well-drained, fertile, ideally humus-rich soil and plenty of sun is the prescription for success. Propagation is by cuttings in summer.

Phaedranthus, see *Distictis*.

Pharbitis, see *Ipomoea*.

Phaseolus *Leguminosae*

Only one of the 200 or more species in this mainly tropical American genus is widely used as an ornamental, though several are grown for food, including the decorative scarlet runner bean, *P. coccineus*.

P. caracalla (Zone 9, Zone 5 as annual) (Snail flower) comes from S America and is widely distributed there. It twines upwards to at least 5 m with trifoliate leaves and short axillary racemes of incredibly coiled and twisted flowers. Each of the latter is about 4 cm long, opening creamy-white with purple markings. Within a few hours of opening the white turns to orange-yellow and the purple strengthens slightly. In basic form the flower is pea-shaped and like that of the

123

familiar scarlet runner bean, but both standard and keel petals are elongated and coiled. Culture is as for *Dolichos*.

Pileostegia *Hydrangeaceae*

Three species names can be found for this E Asian genus but only one plant appears to be in cultivation. Botanically, this one species at least, *P. viburnoides* (Zone 7), is inseparable from *Schizophragma* (q.v.) but for its evergreen leaves. It is a self-clinging root climber to 15 m in the wilds of Assam, China and Taiwan, but not more than half this height in Britain. It has pairs of narrowly oval to obovate leaves 6-13 cm in length. They are normally deep green and somewhat corrugated; a nice foil for the flattened, 10-15 cm wide heads of tiny creamy-white flowers which appear in autumn. It needs a site with some sun to flower well and makes a fine specimen for a west wall or sheltered east one. It is said also to thrive on sheltered north walls. Any fertile, moisture-retentive soil is suitable. Propagation is by cuttings in late summer or layering in spring.

Plumbago *Plumbaginaceae*

Depending on the botanical authority there are 12 to 20 species in this widespread genus. Most are shrubs; a few are scramblers, including the well known *P. auriculata* (Zone 9) (*capensis*) from S Africa. Evergreen and slender stemmed, this charming plant can attain at least 4 m in height, probably more, but always needs tying to its support. The 5-12 cm oval leaves are somewhat wavy and taper to the stem where they are joined by two ear-shaped stipules — hence the 'new' name *auriculata*. During summer and autumn the ever-branching stems terminate in clusters of 3-4 cm long flowers like sky-blue primroses. Ordinary soil and half-day sun will ensure a rewarding display of flowers. It stands hard pruning and is best spurred back to the main stems annually in spring. Propagation is by seeds in spring or cuttings in summer.

Podranea *Bignoniaceae*

Two southern African species form this genus, only one of which is widely grown and that not much in Britain. *Podranea* is derived as an anagram of *Pandorea* and it was formerly included in that genus (also earlier, in *Tecoma* and *Bignonia*). *P. ricasoliana* (Zone 9) is modelled on the lines of *Pandorea jasminoides*, but the leaves have seven to eleven leaflets and the fragrant rose-pink, darker-veined flowers have 2 cm long bell-shaped, greenish-white calyces. Although this lovely climber is widely cultivated in the tropics, I have seen it flowering well in a friend's garden not far from Christchurch, New Zealand. It will, in fact, stand slight frost and is then deciduous. Culture is as for *Pandorea*.

Polygonum (knotweed) *Polygonaceae*

Botanical authorities are undecided on species numbers in this worldwide genus, 300 and 150 being the upper and lower limits. Very few are climbers and even fewer have garden worthiness. Those described grow in ordinary soil and need half-day sun really to flower well. Propagation is by cuttings from spring to late summer.

P. aubertii (Zone 4) (*Bilderdykia* and *Fallopia aubertii*) (silver lace vine) comes from West China and Tibet and to the uninitiated looks just like the Russian vine *P. baldschuanicum*. The two are much confused in British gardens. Both are deciduous twiners growing to 20 m or so with ovate to lanceolate 4-10 cm long leaves and plumy panicles of tiny white, bell-shaped flowers. In *P. aubertii* the flower stalks and larger branches of the panicles bear tiny, rough hairs which, though hard to see, can be felt with thumb and forefinger. The panicles also tend to be narrower and stiffer than those of *baldschuanicum*.

P. baldschuanicum (Zone 4) (*Bilderdykia* and *Fallopia baldschuanicum*) (Russian vine) is native to South Tadzhikistan, USSR, and is the familiar climber used to cover unsightly buildings and high fences. It also looks splendid covering a tree. The basic description is covered under *aubertii* except that the flowers are often, but not invariably, pink-tinted and the flower stalks are smooth. It is less common in British gardens than *aubertii*. Both can be aptly described as mile-a-minute vines and should not be planted in small gardens.

P. multiflorum (Zone 7-8) (China, Taiwan) is a tuberous-rooted perennial twiner growing to 4 m or so with red stems and glossy dark green heart-shaped leaves. Panicles of tiny white flowers open in summer. It needs a sheltered, sunny site.

Pueraria (kudzu vine) *Leguminosae*

This genus is an ally of *Phaseolus* (scarlet runner, haricot and French beans). Two of the 15 species are grown as fodder plants, to control erosion and for ornamental purposes. Of these, one only is sometimes grown in Britain and other temperate countries. *P. lobata* (Zone 7-8) (*thunbergiana*) is native to China, Japan and Korea. It is a woody-based, hairy perennial sending out stems to 6 m or more in length which trail or twine, depending on the situation. The trifoliate leaves consist of broadly ovate to rhomboidal leaflets to 15 cm long and are quite handsome viewed *en masse*. In late summer, axillary racemes to 30 cm in length appear bearing fragrant, red-purple pea flowers 1.5-2 cm long. Slender, hairy 10 cm pods follow. During hard winters the stems are killed back, growth resuming from the base. A sunny site is required and ordinary soil. Propagation is by seeds or division in spring or cuttings in summer.

Figure 5.18
Rhodochiton
atrosanguineum

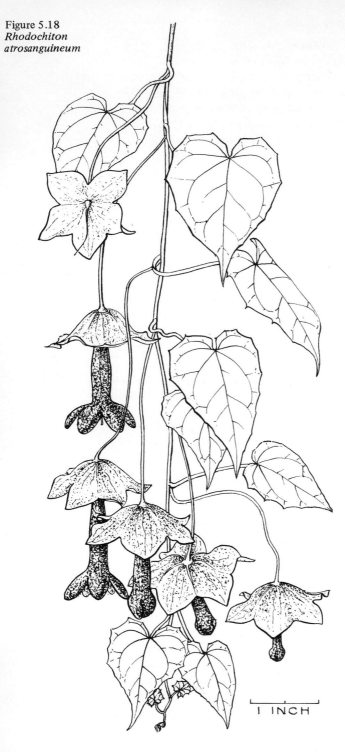

I INCH

Pyrostegia (golden shower) *Bignoniaceae*

Of the four or five species credited to this genus, only one is widely cultivated. This is *P. venusta* (Zone 9-10) (*Bignonia venusta*) from Brazil. A vigorous tendril climber growing to at least 10 m it also happily trails along the ground and efficiently covers unsightly banks. Unlike many climbers it also flowers well in this supine state. The leaves are composed of two ovate, stalked leaflets 5-8 cm long. In late winter and spring all the upper leaf axils bear stalked clusters of tubular 5-6 cm long flowers of a beautiful shade of glowing golden-orange. A big plant pouring out of a tree or clothing a high wall, particularly if backlit by a low sun, provides one of the spectacles of the climbing plant world. Ordinary fertile soil and sun are needed. Propagation is by cuttings in summer.

Rhodochiton *Scrophulariaceae*

R

The one Mexican species in this genus, *R. atrosanguineum* (Zone 9) (*R. volubile*), is allied to *Asarina* and is identical in mode of growth. It is an evergreen perennial with somewhat woody main stems and rich green heart-shaped leaves, the long stalks of which act as tendrils. In flower it looks to be far removed from *Asarina*. Each pendent flower has a widely expanded, broadly five-lobed red calyx rather like a coolie's hat. From the centre of this hangs the deep purple-red tubular 3.5-4.5 cm long corolla, its tip expanded into five blunt petal lobes. A plant well hung with flowers is an intriguing and charming sight. With adequate warmth it flowers for most of the year. Plants from seeds sown in early spring will flower the same year. Ordinary soil and at least partial sun are its modest requirements. Propagation is by seed.

Rosa (rose) *Rosaceae*

Depending on the botanical authority there are between 100 and 250 species of rose. All but a few are found in the northern temperate zone, the remainder in mountains to the south. The generally prickly stems, pinnate leaves and wide open five-petalled flowers are typical characters of all wild roses, as are the rounded to flask-shaped fruits known as hips or heps. Comparatively few rose species are climbers or scramblers and of these even fewer are widely cultivated. There are, however, numerous hybrids and cultivars of complex hybrid origin which can be grown as climbers. Some of the best of these are described below, but the selection must, for reasons of room, be a personal one. Most ordinary soils are suitable for roses, especially if enriched with manure or some other humus source. Most species and cultivars prefer full to half-day sun, but a few will tolerate more shade. Mention of this is made in the individual descriptions. For the purposes of pruning, climbing roses can be divided

127

into two groups, wild species and garden hybrids. The species do not need any regular pruning, but if grown on walls some thinning may be needed, removing old and twiggy stems and branches that flower poorly or not at all. The garden hybrids can be sub-divided into climbers and ramblers. Climbers benefit from regular pruning. Old and twiggy stems should be cut out annually in late winter and all lateral flowering stems cut back to two to four buds. If the rose is repeat flowering, the removal of stems that have bloomed should be done as soon as the last petals fall. If it is a once only flowerer it can be left until late winter. Ramblers should be pruned immediately after flowering, the stems that have bloomed being cut out near ground level or at their junction with the parent stem. At this time (late summer) the new stems will be well grown and should be tied in to the pillar support to replace those removed. Some so-called ramblers, e.g. 'Alberic Barbier', are midway between climbers and true ramblers. They tend to produce fewer basal stems each year and will bloom a second season on the first year flowering stems. Pruning consists of removing some of the two and three-year-old stems annually. All climbing roses can be propagated by soft or semi-hardwood cuttings in summer under glass or by hardwood cuttings outside in late autumn, ideally *in situ*.

R. X 'Alister Stella Gray' ('Golden Rambler') was raised in the USA in 1894. It is a climber growing to 5 m with glossy leaves and clusters of double, fragrant, 6-8 cm wide flowers from mid-summer to late autumn. Each bud starts rich yellow and as it opens out flat, changes to cream.

R. X 'Aloha' is a short pillar rose growing to 2.5 m in height. It was raised in 1949 from 'Mercedes Gallart' X 'New Dawn' and is more of a lax shrub than a true climber. The dark glossy foliage nicely backs the large, clear rose-pink flowers with their delightful tea-scent.

R. X 'Alberic Barbier' originated in 1900 from crossing the small yellow Tea rose 'Shirley Hibberd' by *R. wichuraiana*. It is still one of the finest Ramblers (really a semi-Rambler) with handsome lustrous foliage and clusters of deep cream, pointed buds which expand to double, apple-scented, cream flowers. After the main summer blooming, odd flower clusters are produced until late autumn. Well-grown specimens can exceed 6 m in height.

R. X 'Albertine' was raised in 1921 from *R. wichuraiana* by the coppery Hybrid Tea Rose 'Mrs A.R. Waddell'. Really a great sprawling bush to 2 m high by 5 m wide, it is more easily managed as a climber and can then exceed 6 m on a wall. The glossy leaves go nicely with the coppery-pink buds and purer pink open flowers which expand around mid-summer. Unfortunately the stems are fiercely prickly but this is a small price to pay for such a strikingly lovely rose.

R. X 'American Pillar' is a triple hybrid between *R. wichuraiana*, *R. setigera* and an unnamed red Hybrid Perpetual. A very strong growing Rambler it has good glossy foliage and a profusion of intense pink, single flowers with a white eye, in summer.

R. X *anemoneflora* (Zone 7) (*R. triphylla*) has trifoliate leaves, not a common character among roses in general. It is a double flowered hybrid direct from Chinese gardens, being introduced to Britain in 1884. Of unknown parentage, it has obvious affinities with *R. banksiae*, with other characters possibly from *R. laevigata* and *R. multiflora*. A Rambler in habit it bears clusters of small, fully double flowers which open pink and fade to almost white. It needs a sheltered, sunny wall.

R. X *anemonoides* (*R. sinica* 'Anemone') was raised in Germany about 1895, but its parentage was either unknown or not recorded. It leans much towards *R. laevigata* in appearance but bears 10 cm wide clear pink, single flowers with a darker veining. A Tea Rose is presumably the other parent of this charming but vigorous, 5 m tall hybrid. 'Ramona' is a deeper coloured sport which arose in California in 1913.

R. arvensis (Zone 6) (field rose) is native to southern and western Europe including Britain. It is a trailing or mound-building shrub with prominently green, slender stems, bright green leaves and pure white single flowers. In the past it has entered into the parentage of several rambling roses, notably a group of double cultivars known as Ayrshire roses. Most of these are now either lost, or found occasionally in the collections of specialists. The double white 'Venusta Pendula' has been available in recent years. Well worth looking out for is 'Splendens' with semi-double cream flowers, reddish in bud, and having a sweetly aromatic fragrance that has earned for it the name 'Myrrh-scented rose'.

R. banksiae (China) can climb to 10 m in height given the chance, but can easily be kept to a third of this. Frequently known simply as the Banksian rose it comes in a variety of forms. Basically it is a bushy climber with almost prickleless stems, leaves of three to five smooth leaflets and clusters of small white or yellow flowers in early summer. It needs a sheltered, sunny wall to thrive and flower well. The wild single white is known as *R. banksiae normalis* and has a delightful scent of violets. *R. b.* 'Lutescens' has single flowers a little less strongly scented. *R. b.* 'Lutea' is the Yellow Banksian and the most widely and successfully grown in Britain. It has double yellow blooms, unfortunately only slightly fragrant. The original form to be introduced was a double white and as it is the botanical species type is now designated *R. b. banksiae*, though better known as *R. b.* 'Alba Plena'. It also has the violet scent.

R. bracteata (Zone 8) (Macartney rose) was introduced from China in 1793 by Lord Macartney, head of the British mission there, though actually collected by Sir George Staunton (for whom *Stauntonia* is named). Almost evergreen, it has rich, lustrous foliage formed of uniquely blunt-tipped leaflets. From mid-summer to autumn, pure white, 10 cm wide lemon-scented flowers emerge from a cluster of ovate, coarsely-fringed, downy bracts. It needs a sheltered warm wall to flower well. In southern USA it has become locally naturalised.

R. brunonii (Zone 8) (Himalayan musk rose) has a wide native range, from Afghanistan through the Himalayas to western China. It is vigorous, reaching to 12 m or more in a tree. The 15-20 cm long leaves may be glossy but are usually matt and with a greyish cast. In mild climates they are semi-evergreen. In summer, large, more or less conical trusses of yellow-budded white flowers, each 4-5 cm wide, open and exhale a musky fragrance. It has been confused with *R. moschata*, but that species is no more than a tall shrub with dark green leaves and larger flowers having petals with slender pointed tips (those of *brunonii* are blunt).

R. canina (Zone 4) (Europe, W Asia) is the familiar pink dog rose or common brier of hedgerows and thickets. It is usually a tall shrub but can scramble to 5 m or so into a tree. It has entered into the parentage of some climbing hybrid cultivars, e.g. the primrose-scented almost single white Rambler 'Una'.

R. X 'Cecile Brunner Climbing' ('Climbing Bloomfield Abundance') can reach 6 m on a tree or high wall but is easily kept to half this height. The original bush from which it sported in 1894, reaches only 1.2 m and arose from crossing the old Tea rose 'Mme de Tartas' with an unnamed seedling Poly-pom (Dwarf Polyantha). Also sometimes known as 'Mignon' and the 'Sweetheart Rose' it bears clusters of the most exquisitely formed little clear pink flowers just like those of a miniature Hybrid Tea. It is also sweetly scented and produces a few clusters of flowers into the autumn after the main summer display.

R. X 'Chaplin's Pink Climber' was raised in 1928 from 'Paul's Scarlet' X 'American Pillar'. A rambler attaining 3 m in height, with good glossy foliage, its pink, semi-double flowers are almost too intense a shade for peace of mind. Nevertheless it is a vigorous, showy rose and still quite popular.

R. chinensis (Zone 7) (China rose) is, in its native China, a very changeable species, varying from small shrubs to quite tall scramblers. It has scattered prickles and leaves composed of three to five slender-pointed glossy leaflets. The clustered flowers vary from pink to crimson or scarlet and single to semi-double. The Chinese garden forms produce a succession of flowers once they start and this

130

so-called recurrent character has played a vital role in all modern roses, including the Climbers.

R. X *cooperi* or 'Cooper's Burmese' was collected as seed in the wild but the only plant raised and now grown under this name appears to be a hybrid, probably between *R. gigantea* and *laevigata*. It has very glossy, handsome foliage and single, pure white flowers to 10 cm wide. It needs a warm sheltered wall.

R. X 'Crimson Shower' was raised in 1951 as a seedling from 'Excelsa' ('Red Dorothy Perkins'). A tall Rambler to 5 m, it is distinct in not opening its crimson, rosetted-double flowers until the later part of the summer and continuing well into autumn.

R. X 'Cupid' is a thorny beauty growing to 5 m. A climber of Hybrid Tea style, its parentage is not disclosed. It was raised in 1915 by B.R. Cant. The almost single flowers are large and pale peach-pink and fragrant. After the one big show of blossom there is a crop of large, rounded, orange-red hips.

R. X 'Danse du Feu' ('Spectacular') resulted from the cross 'Paul's Scarlet' X a *multiflora* seedling. A Climber, it grows to 3 m and has large, handsome leaves and orange-scarlet double flowers that open out flat and have a slight scent.

R. X 'Debutante' has the deep pink Hybrid Perpetual 'Baroness Rothschild' as one parent and the glossy-leaved *R. wichuraiana* as the other. It grows to 5 m and is perhaps the best clear pink, double-flowered Rambler.

R. X 'Dr van Fleet' is the slightly more vigorous climber from which 'New Dawn' sprang as a recurrent, flowering mutation (sport). It was raised in the USA in 1910 by Dr W. van Fleet by crossing *R. wichuraiana* X 'Safrano' X 'Souvenir du President Carnot'. It can climb to 6 m and freely bears its delightful sprays of double, pale pink, scented flowers against glossy foliage, around mid-summer.

R. X 'Dorothy Perkins' bears large clusters of what are sometimes described as shocking pink flowers. Although still seen around it is very prone to mildew and has been superseded by better things, e.g. 'Debutante'.

R. X 'Dream Girl' is a seedling from 'Dr van Fleet'. It is a short climber to 3 m and ideal on a pillar. The large, fully double, fragrant flowers are coral-pink, fading gracefully as they age. The dark, lustrous foliage makes a good backing.

R. X 'Easlea's Golden Rambler' behaves much more like a once blooming climber. Growing to 5 m it has distinctive, deep glossy, corrugated foliage and almost double 11.5 cm wide rich creamy yellow flowers, darker in bud, with a boss of golden stamens and a strong fragrance. It was raised in 1932.

R. X 'Emily Gray' arose in 1918 from crossing the creamy-yellow Rambler 'Jersey Beauty' with the China shrub rose 'Comtesse du

Cayla', a chameleon in shifting shades of copper, coral and salmon-pink. A vigorous grower, it is a climber to 6 m with fragrant, buff-yellow almost single flowers of good fragrance.

R. X 'Felicité et Perpétue' has been delighting us since 1827 when it was raised by M Jacques, gardener to the Duc d'Orléans. It has neat, lustrous foliage on bushy stems 3-4 m tall and double, rosette-formed creamy-white flowers from pink-tinted buds. There is a light scent reminiscent of primroses. In sheltered sites it is partially ever-green, being descended from the evergreen R. *sempervirens*. The etymology of the name is in some question. Despite the stories of St Felicitas and St Perpetua as an inspiration for the name, the original rendering appears always to have been without the 'et'. The matter has been researched in some detail by Elspeth Napier, editor of the RHS *The Garden*, (see the publication for August 1982, p. 336). The theme of the name would seem to be 'perpetual Felicity', perhaps referring to its semi-evergreen nature. Whatever the name this is a first-rate rose, thriving on north walls and in windy upland gardens.

R. *filipes* (Zone 6) (China) will ramp away to 10 m or more and when well established can produce shoots up to 6 m in one season. These robust stems are fiercely prickly but clad with elegant lightish green foliage formed of narrow slender-pointed leaflets. The pale cream, cupped, scented flowers are carried in trusses up to 45 cm long and a large plant creates a spectacle worth travelling far to see. In Britain it is represented by the clone 'Kiftsgate' named after the garden in Gloucestershire where the original and largest plant in the country grows.

R. X 'Francis E. Lester' arose as a seedling from the Hybrid Musk 'Kathleen'. Growing to 4 m or so it is of bushy growth clad with dark foliage which starts life red-tinted. The trusses of single flowers are pink in bud, opening and ageing to near white in the fashion of apple blossom. They exhale a strong, rich, fruity fragrance which might well be called 'essence of summer'.

R. X. 'François Juranville' is a climber to 8 m and has very sharp, hooked prickles. Nevertheless it has long been a name to reckon with and is a truly lovely rose with its flat, double, apple-scented flowers full of coral-pink petals with a yellow base. It is yet another child of R. *wichuraiana* and was raised in 1906.

R. *gigantea* (Zone 7-8) (Burma, W China) is a climber to at least 10 m, but in Britain needs a really warm, sheltered wall to grow satisfactorily. In the wild it is a true giant, climbing to tops of trees 20-25 m tall. It has large leaves and single, fragrant, white flowers up to 14 cm wide. The big hips are like crab apples.

R. X 'Golden Showers' grows 2-3 m tall and makes a good pillar rose. In reality it is more like a tall, erect shrub. The foliage is substantial and glossy, making a good accompaniment for the large, double, fragrant, light yellow flowers. It is repeat flowering.

R. X 'Goldfinch' looks much like *R. multiflora* and grows like a Rambler with clusters of semi-double flowers that are buff-apricot yellow in bud and, on opening, age almost white. There is a delightful fruity fragrance suggesting bananas and oranges blended together. It is a once flowerer and was raised in 1907.

R. X 'Guinée' is darkest crimson bordering on maroon, and repeat flowering. Each bloom is a shapely double and richly old fashioned rose scented. It was raised in 1938 from 'Souvenir de Claudius Denoyel' X 'Ami Quinard' and has good foliage. Of climbing habit it can reach 5 m in good soil.

R. X 'Handel' is a climber of Hybrid Tea form, raised by Sam McGredy from 'Columbine' X 'Heidelberg' in 1965. Erect in habit, it has good dark foliage and clusters of double, but open-centred, flowers from shapely buds. The wavy petals are creamy-white with an edging of deep pink which often suffuses throughout. The degree of colouring seems to depend on temperature and soil moisture.

R. helenae (Zone 6) (China) is rather like *R. filipes* but less vigorous and with smaller flower clusters. The hips are a richer orange-red and more obviously decorative.

R. X 'Kew Rambler' is derived from *R. soulieana* X 'Hiawatha' (a crimson, white-eyed Rambler). It has grey-green foliage and light pink flowers with a basal white zone and yellow stamen cluster. They have the fruity scent of *R. multiflora*. Although a rambler, it can reach 5-6 m in height.

R. laevigata (Zone 7-8) (China, Taiwan to Burma) climbs to 6 m or more, holding on securely with its sharp, reddish-brown hooked prickles set on smooth, green stems. The lustrous leaves are mainly trifoliate, each leaflet ovate to lance-shaped and 4-10 cm long. Pure white and fragrant, each 7-10 cm wide flower is borne solitarily and is followed by a bristly red hip. In Britain it needs a sunny wall to flower well, and when so doing is a most attractive rose. It appears to have been introduced into southern USA around 1780 and quickly made itself at home, becoming naturalised in the surrounding countryside. So much of a wild plant did it become that it acquired the vernacular name of Cherokee rose and was chosen as the State Flower of Georgia.

R. X 'Lawrence Johnston' ('Hidcote Yellow') was raised in 1923 by Pernet-Ducher, from *R. foetida persiana* X 'Madame Eugène Verdier'. It was not put on the market and remained in the nursery until seen and purchased by Major Lawrence Johnston, owner of Hidcote Maner, Gloucestershire. There it became known as 'Hidcote Yellow'. Graham S. Thomas saw it and asked Major Johnston if he could exhibit it at an RHS Show. At the Major's request it was shown under his name and received an Award of Merit in 1948. It is a strong grower to 10 m with good foliage and rich canary-yellow semi-double flowers, exhaling a rich fragrance.

R. X 'Leontine Gervais' is described as a rambler but grows 7-8 m in height. It is much like 'François Juranville', but there is copper and orange shading in the double flowers.

R. longicuspis (*R. lucens*) (China) makes a trio with *R. filipes* and *helenae* and is rather like the latter, but has semi-evergreen, somewhat longer leaves and larger flowers.

R. luciae (Japan) is very much like the more widely grown *R. wichuraiana*, but has leaves with rarely more than five thinner-textured, less glossy leaflets, and flowers 2.5-3 cm wide.

R. X 'Madame Gregoire Staechelin' ('Spanish Beauty') combines the best of 'Frau Karl Druschki' and 'Château de Clos Vougeot' and is the most glorious wall rose of all. Very vigorous, it reaches 6-7 m in two to three years and then produces an abundance of large, nodding, semi-double, glowing pink flowers with a scent of sweet peas. It gives one great show in early summer providing the spectacle of the season. The large leaves are semi-evergreen in a mild winter. It grows well in all aspects, even on a north wall.

R. X 'Meg' was derived in 1954 from that lovely old Hybrid Tea rose 'Madame Butterfly' and it shows in the large, single to semi-double flowers of salmon-yellow and blush pink. The other parent is apparently not known for sure, but seems to be 'Paul's Lemon Pillar' (q.v.) a large-flowered climber of quality. 'Meg' is vigorous, growing to 3 m or so, with a bushy habit and good foliage. It is slightly recurrent after the main gorgeous display.

R. X 'Mermaid' is a child of *R. bracteata* crossed with a double yellow Tea rose. It is another of the British rose breeder William Paul's triumphs and was raised in 1918. A vigorous climber to 7 m or more, it has lustrous foliage and a succession of soft, canary-yellow, five-petalled flowers with a boss of amber stamens which remain fresh for sometime after the petals fall. Providing the site is sheltered, it will grow even on a north wall, but is best in sun.

R. moschata, see under *R. brunonii*.

R. multiflora (Japan, Korea, northern China) is the archetypal rambler and, in one way or another, has lent its habit of growth to all the true Rambler roses. Despite this it can be grown as a large, lax shrub or a climber and is generally described in the latter category. It produces plenty of very long, often only sparingly thorny stems to 3 m or so each year. These are clad with lightish, semi-lustrous leaves, and the second year are wreathed for most of their length with trusses of white flowers. The latter are small but have a disproportionate fruity fragrance. This very easily grown rose is used as a rootstock for budding Hybrid Tea roses and Floribunda. It also makes a good tough hedge. In recent years it has been grown in this way by roadsides and to divide the two lanes of dual carriage-ways, not just for its beauty but because its tough, resilient growth will hold an out-of-control car.

R. X 'New Dawn' arose in USA in 1930 and is a recurrent flowered mutant of 'Dr van Fleet' (q.v.).

R. X *odorata* (*R. chinensis* X *gigantea*) arose in China in early times. Cultivars of this origin are the so-called Tea roses and are seldom grown today. Sometimes seen in collections is 'Fortune's Double Yellow' originally known as *R. odorata pseudindica*, as 'Beauty of Glazenwood' and 'Gold of Ophir'. It grows to about 3 m and bears slightly nodding large, double, coppery-yellow fragrant flowers with a crimson flush. It was found in a Mandarin's garden at Ningpo by the plant collector Robert Fortune in 1845 and for a time was popular in Britain. It needs a warm wall to thrive and flower well.

R. X 'Parade' is the child of 'New Dawn' and the climbing mutant of 'Minna Kordes' ('World's Fair' in USA), a crimson Hybrid Polyantha of 1938 vintage. 'Parade' was raised in 1953. It can achieve 4 m in height as a climber and bears two crops of fragrant, rich carmine, cupped flowers against deep glossy green foliage.

R. X 'Paul Lédé Climbing' is the 5 m tall sport of the original bush Tea rose raised in 1902. Of vigorous growth and with good foliage, it bears a continuous succession of large full-petalled pale buff flowers flushed carmine in the centre. There is a rich Tea rose fragrance, especially noticeable on warm days.

R. X 'Paul's Lemon Pillar' sprang from 'Frau Karl Druschki' X 'Maréchal Niel', both roses of early Hybrid Tea form. It is a climber to 6 m with good foliage and one superb crop of very large, pale lemon-yellow, strongly fragrant flowers soon after mid-summer. It is sometimes listed simply as 'Lemon Pillar'.

R. X 'Paul's Scarlet Climber' is still perhaps the most frequently seen of red climbing roses. About 4 m or more in height it bears a big crop of bright crimson-scarlet flowers around mid-summer. If pruned immediately after the last petals fall, some later blooms can be expected.

R. X 'Pink Perpétue' arose in 1965 from 'Danse du Feu' X 'New Dawn'. Although a vigorous climber it seldom exceeds 2.5 m and makes a fine pillar rose. Of recurrent blooming habit, it produces medium-sized double flowers of bright rose-pink against abundant dark, lustrous foliage.

R. 'Polyantha Grandiflora' is usually listed in nurserymen's catalogues as *R. gentiliana*. Both in their way are wrong, but this is not the place to go into technical and involved details. Suffice it to say that the plant in cultivation is a climber growing to 6 m or so, with sparingly prickly stems, lustrous, handsome foliage, and soon after mid-summer, large trusses of 2.5 cm wide, strongly fragrant white flowers. A good crop of orange-red hips usually follows. It may be a hybrid of *R. moschata* and *multiflora*.

R. X 'Rambling Rector' is essentially a semi-double *R. multiflora* but even more floriferous and fragrant.

R. X 'Ramona', see *R.* X *anemonoides*.

R. X 'Royal Gold' ('Goldilocks Climbing' X 'Lydia') is a 3 m pillar rose with bright, rich, golden-yellow flowers of Hybrid Tea style. It is perpetual flowering and a real eye-catcher when doing well. Of American origin (1957), in Britain it is best in a sunny site.

R. rubus (China) was discovered by Augustine Henry about 1886, but not introduced until 1907 when E.H. Wilson visited the area. It is related to *R. helenae* and similar in appearance but with more strongly scented flowers that are yellow in bud, and with dark red fruits.

R. X 'Sander's White' arrived in 1915 and ever since has been a favourite white-flowered Rambler. It grows to 4 m in height, the strong stems bearing bright glossy green foliage and large clusters of semi-double flowers which open out to disclose yellow centres. It is one of the best ramblers for fragrance.

R. setigera (Zone 5) (eastern USA) is the so-called prairie rose and usually more of a bush than a climber. It has long procumbent to arching stems, however, and can hitch itself up into shrubs and small trees, much as the common dog rose, *R. canina*, does. Grown as a climber it can reach 4 m or more in height. It has leaves composed of three to five exceptionally large leaflets with grey undersides and 4.5-7.5 cm wide flowers in clusters. In cultivation in Britain, the mallow-pink form seems to be commonest. In the wild it varies from crimson to white. It flowers later than most species. Being of zone 5 hardiness it has been used by American rose breeders to produce hardy, larger-flowered climbing roses. 'American Pillar' was one of the earliest of this parentage.

R. X 'Seven Sisters' (*R. multiflora platyphylla*) is named for the shades and colours found in a single truss of the small double flowers. They start cerise-purple, then fade by degrees to pink and pale mauve. It is a vigorous rose often exceeding 6 m in height and has good foliage. It was introduced from Japan by Sir Charles Greville around 1816 and appears basically to be a hybrid between *R. multiflora* and *wichuraiana*. Although not really tender it can suffer stem tip damage by early frosts, and is best in a sheltered site.

R. sinica, see *R.* X *anemonoides* and *R. laevigata*.

R. sinowilsonii (China) has been considered as part of *R. longicuspis*, but as seen in cultivation is quite distinct, though obviously closely akin to that species. For a start, the leaves are magnificent, to 30 cm long as against the 20 cm of *longicuspis*. They are a deep shining green and almost evergreen. The flower buds are ovoid (tapered in *longicuspis*) and the stems and thorns are glossy red-brown. Regrettably it is not very hardy and in Britain needs the most sheltered and sunny sites.

R. X 'Soldier Boy' was derived from 'Guinée' by the British rose breeder E.B. le Grice in 1953. A climber to 3 m it bears an eye-stunning shower of brilliant red blossom around mid-summer followed by a scattering of flowers into autumn.

R. soulieana (Zone 7) (China) has fiercely prickly stems and a prodigious rate of growth when established, but even so deserves to be seen more often for its charming soft grey foliage. It is, in fact, the greyest leaved of all roses, a fact seldom lauded even by the experts. It compliments this distinctive foliage with showers of creamy-white, fragrant flowers in summer, often followed by small, orange hips. Often described as a large shrub, it can make shoots 4 m or more in length in a season, and can be trained as wall covering or into a tree.

R. X 'Splendens', see *R. arvensis*.

R. X 'Spanish Beauty', see 'Madame Gregoire Staechelin'.

R. X 'Una', see under *R. canina*.

R. X 'Veilchenblau' was raised as long ago as 1909, yet it has an almost *avant garde* colour. Almost thornless and of Rambler habit, 4-5 m tall, it bears large clusters of small semi-double flowers that start deep magenta and age to lilac, sometimes streaked with white. There is a fruity fragrance reminiscent of oranges.

R. X 'Violette' is similar to 'Veilchenblau', but the flowers age to a greyish-maroon and the scent is much fainter and less fruity; much more attractive than it sounds.

R. X 'Wedding Day' could well have been included under *R. sinowilsonii*, from which species it is derived. It differs in its less magnificent foliage and more freely produced flowers which start as apricot-yellow buds and open creamy-yellow, ageing white. It was raised in 1950 by Sir Frederick Stern of Highdown, Sussex.

R. wichuraiana (Zone 6-7) (China, Japan, Korea, Taiwan) is surprisingly little seen considering its all-pervading influence on rose breeding, especially of Ramblers and other Climbers. It is largely a trailer and scrambler, but though the stems bear few prickles it can hitch up into trees to 4 m or more. The evergreen leaves are small, formed of five to nine leaflets of almost leathery texture but of a satisfyingly polished deep green. It is this foliage character that is so evident in all its hybrid descendants, even when several generations removed from the species. The 4-5 cm flowers are white, delightfully fragrant and appear in trusses in late summer. The hips are dark red. Although most effective as a climber, it makes a decoratively different and quite efficient groundcover.

Rubus (blackberry, raspberry) *Rosaceae*

In the usual concept of a species there are 250 rubi, but if the many microspecies are considered, there are close to 3000. Some of these are scramblers or hook climbers and a few are worth growing purely as ornamentals. They may have simple or compound leaves and small to large clusters of five-petalled flowers. The often edible fruit is an aggregate one, being formed of many single seeded drupelets, e.g. like those of the raspberry. Ordinary fertile soil and sun or partial shade gives good results. Propagation is by division or suckers from autumn to spring, seed when ripe and tip layering in late summer.

R. flagelliflorus (Zone 7) (*R. flagelliformis*) (China) is a slender, evergreen scrambler to 2 m or more, with ovate, long-pointed, often shallowly lobed leaves clad with a fine buff felt beneath and 10-15 cm long. Stems and leaf stalks are only minutely prickly. Small white flowers open in summer and are followed by black edible fruits. It is a handsome foliage plant.

R. henryi (Zone 6) (China) can attain 5 m in height if a suitable bush or low tree is available for support. Like the previous species it is evergreen and grown for its attractive foliage, in this case deeply three-lobed and white felted beneath. The small and rather mean little flowers are sometimes followed by glossy black fruits. *R. h. bambusarum* differs in having the leaves cut into three distinct leaflets.

R. ichangensis (Zone 6) (China) was considered by its introducer, E.H. Wilson to be one of the finest for its fruits. Following the small white flowers they are red, of good flavour and carried in long panicles 30-60 cm in length. The semi-evergreen leaves too are appealing, 8-17 cm long, leathery and glossy, oblong-ovate with a prominent heart-shaped base and tapered point. Such prickles as there are are minute. For some years it has been rare in Britain, but with the recent lifting of the 'bamboo curtain' it has been re-introduced by Roy Lancaster and others. It is none too hardy in Britain and needs a sheltered spot.

R. laciniatus (Zone 4) (*R. fruticosus laciniatus*) has acquired the apt vernacular names cut, fern and parsley-leaved blackberry. Its provenance is unknown, but it is basically of mutant origin from one of the *fruticosus* microspecies. In one of its cultivar selections, such as 'Oregon Thornless', it is often grown in the fruit garden. The finely cut leaves, however, are decidedly decorative and make it one of those useful dual purpose plants. Trained to a pillar it will grace any shrub or mixed bed or border.

R. lambertianus (Zone 6) (China) is another E.H. Wilson intro-duction (1907) with slender, angled, prickly stems and glossy green leaves 7-13 cm in length. The latter vary greatly from simple and ovate to shallowly three or five-lobed. Small white flowers are followed by red fruits.

R. lineatus (Zone 8) (Himalayas, China, Malaysia) is semi-evergreen or deciduous to about 3 m in height. It must rank as one of the most attractive of all foliage brambles, with digitate leaves reminiscent of horse chestnut. Each leaf has five oblanceolate saw-toothed leaflets 10-20 cm or more in length. The upper surfaces are dark green with a contrasting white line of down along the midribs. The under-surfaces are silky-white downy. Both flowers and fruits are small, the former white, the latter red or yellow.

R. parkeri (Zone 6) (China) has deciduous, simple leaves, 10-17 cm long, broadly lance-shaped with a cordate base, a long tapered point and a covering beneath of reddish-brown hair. Small white flowers are followed by black, early ripening fruits.

R. phoenicolasius (Zone 5) (China, Japan, Korea) is the Japanese wineberry and well worth growing for fruit and ornament. Having stems to 3 m or so, thickly set with red bristles, it bears trifoliate leaves 13 cm or more long, the leaflets of which are broad and white-felted beneath. The flowers have small pink petals but intriguingly long tapered sepals covered with glandular red hairs. They are followed by conical red fruits about 2 cm long which, though sweet and juicy, rather lack flavour.

R. ulmifolius (Zone 4) (Europe, east to Yugoslavia, NW Africa, Macronesia) is one of the microspecies of the common blackberry *R. fruticosus*. It is one of the most widespread in Britain and very distinctive with its smallish three to five dark green leaflets, thinly white-felted below, and purplish-pink flowers. It is not worth garden room for ornamental purposes, but its cultivar 'Bellidiflorus' most certainly is. Here, each flower is formed of numerous narrow petals and looks like a pompon. A plant in full bloom is a most attractive and eye-catching sight. What a pity then, that this species is so vigorous and sharply prickly. 'Variegatus' is a foliage bramble, the main veins of each leaflet picked out in yellow, but there are more kindly disposed variegated climbers if such are required.

Sandersonia *Liliaceae*

S

This S African species contains one species, *S. aurantiaca* (Zone 9) from Natal. In growth habit it could be mistaken for a small *Gloriosa*, having similar but slightly narrower and often hook-tipped leaves on stems up to 60 cm tall. The flowers, however, are totally different, broadly urn-shaped, about 2.5-3 cm and a lovely shade of clear orange. It makes a charming pot plant for the greenhouse or sun room. Culture as for *Gloriosa*.

Schisandra *Schisandraceae*

About 25 species form this E Asian and eastern North American genus. They are stem twiners with simple alternate leaves, and unisexual flowers generally on separate plants (dioecious). One to several flowers are borne in the leaf axils, each one being bowl-shaped and formed of up to 16 tepals. The fruit is an aggregate one, comparable to that of a blackberry or raspberry. An ordinary humus-enriched soil is suitable, preferably in partial shade though full sun is tolerated. Propagation is by cuttings in late summer.

S. chinensis (Zone 5) (China, Japan, Korea, Sakhalin) is a vigorous, deciduous species growing to 10 m or so with 5-10 cm long elliptic to obovate leaves carried on red stems. The 1-2 cm wide white to pale pink, fragrant flowers are borne in clusters of two to three in late spring. Spike-like red fruit clusters, 5-15 cm long develop if both male and female plants are present and persist well into the winter.

S. grandiflora (Zone 7) (Himalayas) grows 6 m or more, its deciduous, obovate leaves being up to 13 cm long. Solitary, pale pink flowers 2.5-3 cm wide open in early summer. *S. g. rubriflora* is still often listed as a species in its own right — *S. rubriflora*. Without doubt it is the finest of all the schisandras having deep crimson flowers with the same sort of appeal as *Berberidopsis*. The red fruiting clusters are 6-15 cm long.

S. propinqua (Zone 8-9) (Himalayas) comes from fairly low altitudes in the Himalayas and needs greenhouse treatment in Britain. A vigorous evergreen plant to 10 m or so, it has ovate, lance-shaped leaves 5-13 cm long and greenish-yellow and orange flowers about 1 cm wide in autumn. The scarlet fruits are up to 15 cm long. *S. p. chinensis* (Zone 7-8) (*sinensis*) is a hardier Chinese version with narrower leaves and yellower flowers.

S. sphenanthera (Zone 6) (China) has warty stems and 1 cm wide terracotta-coloured flowers in early summer, otherwise it is much like *S. grandiflora*.

Schizophragma *Hydrangeaceae*

Two E Asian species form this genus of deciduous root climbers. They differ from the very closely allied *Hydrangea* in having what appears to be broadly ovate bracts around the flattened flower clusters. Anatomically, however, each bract is the sepal of a sterile flower and comparable to the four-sepalled ones of *Hydrangea*. Ordinary soil and a site in at least half-day sun will ensure a good display of flowers though it will grow on sunless north walls. Propagation is by seed or layering in spring or cuttings in late summer, ideally with bottom heat 18°-21°C.

S. hydrangeoides (Zone 5) (Japan, Korea) can attain 15 m in the wild, its robust stems clinging firmly to the bark of whatever tree it scales. The 10-15 cm broadly ovate leaves have a heart-shaped base and angular teeth. They are dark green above and pale, almost glaucous beneath. The individual cream flowers are tiny but carried in flat, lacy clusters, 20-25 cm wide, the margins of which bear 2.5-4 cm long cream 'bracts'. In the highly desirable *S. h.* 'Roseum' the bracts are pink suffused. Although most effective in the garden as a wall plant, *S. hydrangeoides* looks very attractive climbing up a tree, particularly if there are no low branches to obstruct the view of it when in full bloom. In its homeland it is not infrequent in mountain woods, where, in company with *Hydrangea anomala petiolaris*, it behaves just like common ivy, running up almost every tree and when in flower creating a sight to remember.

S. integrifolium (Zone 7) is the Chinese version of *hydrangeoides*, with larger, toothless or sparingly toothed leaves and much bigger flower clusters with 'bracts' 5-8 cm long.

Senecio (ragwort) *Compositae*

Variously estimated at between 2000 and 3000 species, this has the distinction of being the largest genus of flowering plants. Not only is it cosmopolitan in distribution, but among the many species are annuals, perennials (including many succulents), shrubs, small trees and climbers. The climbers are stem twiners with lobed or boldly toothed simple leaves and terminal clusters of showy daisy-like flowers. They grow in ordinary soil in a sunny site. In Britain they need frost-free to cool greenhouse conditions. Propagation is by cuttings in summer.

S. confusus (Zone 9) (southern Mexico to Honduras) (Mexican flame vine) can attain several metres in height under ideal conditions, the sinuous stems bearing rather thick-textured, narrowly ovate leaves 4-7 cm in length. The 2-4 cm wide flower heads open in summer, the ray florets starting off orange and ageing red.

S. macroglossus (Zone 9) (South Africa) has acquired the names Cape ivy and wax vine from the shape and texture of its thick, dark green glossy leaves. It is grown largely as a foliage plant throughout the tropics, and as a house plant. The 5 cm wide flowers are yellow, borne solitarily or in small, terminal clusters. A form with white ray florets is grown, and 'Variegatus' has the leaves 50 per cent or more yellow, sometimes also reddish flushed.

S. mikanioides (Zone 8-9) (*S. scandens*) (S Africa) is sometimes called German or parlour ivy, and is the hardiest of the cultivated climbing ragworts. In Britain it survives outside in the warmest areas or during the mildest winters. It can attain at least 6 m in height and has rather ivy-like, somewhat fleshy textured leaves. The small flower heads, which are yellow and lack ray florets, occur in dense,

141

often quite large terminal clusters in autumn.

S. tamoides (Zone 9) (central and southern Africa) climbs 3-5 m in height and bears angularly lobed, somewhat fleshy leaves that are grey-purple tinted and up to 7 cm long. The 3 cm wide bright yellow daisy flowers are carried in profusion from autumn to spring providing a minimum temperature of 7°-10°C can be maintained.

Sicyos *Cucurbitaceae*

Depending upon the botanical authority, there are between 15 and 50 species in this genus of mainly tropical annuals. One only is sometimes grown as a quick summer screen or for botanical interest. *S. angulatus* (Zone 6 as annual) (eastern North America) is the bur or star cucumber, an annual tendril climber to 5 m or so with rounded, sharply five-angled or lobed leaves covered with slightly sticky hairs. Small greenish-white, unisexual flowers appear in clusters in the leaf axils in summer and are followed by bristly-prickly yellow fruits about 12 mm long. Ordinary soil that does not dry out and a site in sun or partial shade are required. Propagation is by seed in spring ideally under glass or *in situ*, when fear of worst frost has passed.

Sinofranchetia *Lardizabalaceae*

One species comprises this genus which in turn, is closely allied to *Holboellia* and *Stauntonia*. *S. chinensis* (Zone 7) (China) is a deciduous twiner to 15 m with trifoliate leaves, the individual leaflets of which are 7-15 cm long, broadly ovate and glaucous beneath. In late spring or early summer small white flowers appear in pendent 10 cm long racemes. They are followed on female plants (even in the absence of a pollinator) by bluish-purple fruits of grape-like size and appearance. This unique climber was introduced by E.H. Wilson and first raised at Kew Gardens in 1908. It has a lot of quiet attraction and deserves to be seen more often. The RHS conferred an Award of Merit in 1948. Culture is as for *Stauntonia*.

Sinomenium *Menispermaceae*

The one species in this genus, *S. acutum*, was formerly included in *Cocculus* and has all the main characteristics of that genus. The botanical division hinges on the stamen number of the male flowers; in *Cocculus* there are three to six, in *Sinomenium*, nine to twelve. *S. acutum* (Zone 7) (E Asia) is a deciduous twiner to 5 m or so with oval to kidney-shaped, lobed or unlobed leaves up to 15 cm long. The small yellow flowers are borne in tapered panicles 15-30 cm long around mid-summer. Black fruits with white waxy patina follow the flowers and when seen in quantity are quite attractive. *S. a. cinereum*, with downy leaves, is the commonest form in cultivation. Culture is as for *Cocculus*.

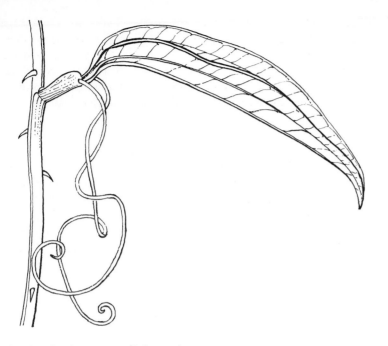

Figure 5.19
A single leaf of
Smilax showing the
tendrils derived
from stipules

Smilax *Smilacacaceae* (*Liliaceae*)

Depending on the classifier, there are between 200 and 350 species in this widespread genus. Most of them are herbaceous or woody-stemmed perennials climbing by means of paired tendrils at the leaf bases which appear to be modified stipules. Some species also have hooked stem prickles. The generally insignificant dioecious flowers are followed by black, purple or red berries. The species described here grow in ordinary soil in sun or partial shade. Propagation is by seed or division in spring.

S. aspera (Zone 7) (Mediterranean area to southern central Asia and Canary Islands) sometimes bears the confusing vernacular name, rough bindweed. An evergreen with prickly stems it tends to form low, tangled thickets rather than climb, though it can do so when given rich soil that does not dry out. The glossy, often pale flecked leaves are variable, from broadly ovate to narrowly triangular, 4-10 cm in length. The small greenish flowers are fragrant and open in summer. Red, glossy berries may follow.

S. china (Zone 6-7) (China, Japan, Korea) has somewhat prickly stems 2-3 m long or more, clad with broadly ovate, deciduous leaves 5-7.5 cm long, some of which redden in autumn. Yellow-green flowers open in late spring and are followed by sizeable red berries. The large, fleshy, edible root ('China root') contains a drug formerly used in the treatment of gout.

S. discotis (Zone 7) (China) is a prickly-stemmed deciduous

143

climber to 5 m in height with ovate leaves 4-9 cm long, the lower surfaces of which are bluish-white tinted. The flowers are yellow-green and the fruits black.

S. excelsa (Zone 6) (E Europe, W Asia) is perhaps the most handsome of all the cultivated smilax species, soaring up into the tops of trees at least 20 m high. The stems bear sharp straight, spine-like prickles and taper-pointed evergreen, or semi-evergreen ovate-cordate leaves to 10 cm long. The flowers appear in summer and are followed by red berries.

S. rotundifolia (Zone 4) (eastern N America) is known as horse brier in its native land. Partially evergreen or deciduous, it can ramble for 4 or 5 m or more, the angular stems bearing a few short prickles. The leaves are widely heart-shaped, up to 15 cm long and glossy on both surfaces. Yellow-green flowers are followed by black berries covered with a waxy white patina. This is the hardiest of the taller smilaxes and worthy of being grown more often.

Figure 5.20
Solandra grandiflora,
see under *S. maxima*

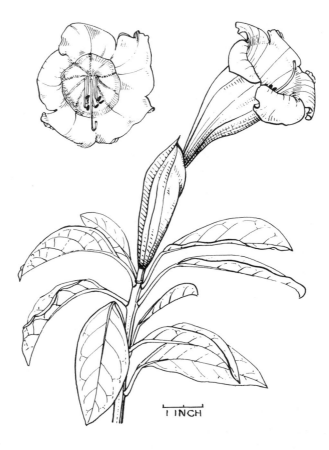

I INCH

Solandra (Capa de Oro) *Solanaceae*

Of the ten species in this genus, only one is really widely cultivated and will thrive under cool greenhouse conditions in Britain. This is *S. maxima* (Zone 9-10) from Mexico, a handsomely rampant ever-green scrambler capable of attaining the tops of trees 50 m in height. It has broadly elliptic glossy leaves and trumpet-shaped flowers up to 18 cm long. The latter are fragrant and open in the evening when they are pale yellow with five broad lobes and five internal dark purple stripes. Quite soon the petal lobes reflex and by the next day the colour is much deeper. By the third day a strong brown suffusion changes the colour to a genuine old gold. Also known as golden chalice vine, this species has been confused with *S. grandiflora* but that species has flowers with smaller petal lobes and ten purple stripes. A sunny site in fertile soil is required and plants under glass should be kept almost dry in winter. Propagation is by cuttings in summer.

Solanum (nightshade) *Solanaceae*

This cosmopolitan genus of 1700 species contains annuals, peren-nials, shrubs and climbers. They have alternate, simple or dissected leaves and clusters of nodding star-shaped flowers with the five stamens united to form a central, generally yellow beak or narrow cone. The fruit is a fleshy berry. The species described here are best in a sunny site and thrive in ordinary soil. Propagation is by seeds under glass or cuttings in late summer.

S. crispum (Zone 8) (Chile, Peru) is a scrambler to 5 m or so with semi-woody stems and ovate leaves to 10 cm or so. The fragrant flowers are rather potato-like, blue-purple and usually borne in abun-dance from late summer to late autumn. It is best on a wall where it needs tying in place, but will ramble through a large shrub or small tree very effectively. In Britain it is almost entirely represented by the cultivar 'Glasnevin' ('Autumnale'), a clone with a long flowering season and possibly hardier than the original introduction.

S. jasminoides (Zone 8-9) (potato vine) (southern Brazil to northern Argentina) has slender stems to 6 m or more and is a true climber, holding on by twining leaf stalks. The ovate leaves may be entire or have an irregular number of small lobes at the base. From summer to autumn a succession of palest blue flower clusters expand, individual blossoms being 2.5 cm wide with five broad lobes. *S. j.* 'Album' has pure white flowers. The small fruits are green, tinted brown.

Sollya *Pittosporaceae*

The two Australian species in this genus are small but highly distinc-tive and attractive evergreen twiners. They are displayed to perfection

145

over a fairly open-habited shrub, e.g. a *Callistemon* (bottlebrush) —
one of their countrymen — but can also be grown up a wigwam of
bushy pea sticks. Humus-rich, well-drained soil gives good results.
Propagation is by seed in spring or cuttings in summer.

S. heterophylla (Zone 9) (*S. fusiformis*) is the aptly named blue-
bell creeper, a slender plant growing to 2 m tall with 5 cm long ovate
to lanceolate pale green leaves and in summer and autumn five-
petalled, nodding, 1 cm long bell-like flowers of sky blue. Purple
berries may follow. This little climber is a real charmer and should
be grown much more often.

S. parviflora (Zone 9) (*S. drummondii*) resembles the previous
species but is somewhat smaller with consistently very narrow leaves
and darker blue flowers.

Stauntonia *Lardizabalaceae*

About 15 species of twiners from E Asia comprise this genus. They
have compound leaves formed of three to seven leaflets, occasionally
only one, and unisexual flowers carried on separate plants (dioecious).
The latter have six petal-like sepals, the true petals being modified to
small nectaries. In the male flowers the six stamens are united. (In
the very closely allied *Holboellia* they are free). In the female flowers
the stamens are reduced to small staminodes and there is a three-
carpelled ovary. After pollination, one, two or all the carpels develop
into fleshy fruits. A sunny site is best though partial shade is satisfactory, and the soil should be moisture retentive but well-drained
and, ideally, humus-rich. Propagation is by cuttings in late summer
or seeds when ripe or spring in a cold frame.

S. coriacea, see *Holboellia coriacea*.

S. hexaphylla (Zone 7) (S Korea, Japan, Ryukyus) produces
vigorous stems to 10 m or so, clad with evergreen leaves composed
of three to seven ovate to elliptic leaflets. The leaflets are dark green,
glossy and leathery, up to 14 cm long. In spring, small clusters of
2 cm white, purple-tinted, fragrant flowers open. If male and female
plants are grown fairly close together, 3-5 cm long egg-shaped,
purple-red fruits develop. A warm summer is needed for this to
happen in Britain. When fully ripe the edible fruits are sweet and
juicy but a bit insipid.

Streptosolen *Solanaceae*

One species, the so-called marmalade bush, *S. jamesonii* (Zone 9-10),
comprises this genus from Colombia and Ecuador. It is a scrambler
often grown as a short term pot plant in the cool greenhouse. In a
tub or planted in a greenhouse border it makes a splendid splash of
colour in late spring and summer. Attaining 2-3 m in height it has
3-5 cm long finely corrugated rich green leaves which make a perfect

foil for the bright and profuse trusses of blossom. Individual flowers are 2.5-3.5 cm long, the basal part narrowly trumpet-shaped then widely flaring to a bright orange mouth. Ordinary fertile soil and a fairly sunny site are required. Propagation is by cuttings in late spring or late summer at 18°-21°C.

Tacsonia, see *Passiflora*.

Tecoma, see *Campsis*.

Tecomanthe *Bignoniaceae*

About 17 species are credited to this genus of evergreen twiners from the SE Pacific region. They have fairly close affinities with *Pandorea*. Only two species are likely to be seen in Britain and none are at present commercially available. A humus-rich soil is necessary and at least half-day sun. *T. speciosa* will thrive in a cool greenhouse. Propagation is by seed in spring or cuttings in late summer, both at not less than 21°C.

T. dendrophila (New Guinea) reaches the top of forest trees in its homeland. It has leaves of three, or sometimes five, oblong leaflets, each with a short, abrupt point and clusters of 10 cm long mauve-pink and pale yellow flowers. Pointed, bean-like pods 20-30 cm long may develop, but seldom on greenhouse specimens.

T. speciosa (Zone 9) (Three Kings Islands, New Zealand) was, incredibly enough, found as recently as 1945 on only one (Great Island) of this small cluster of Pacific Islands north of New Zealand, by Professor G.T.S. Baylis of the University of Otago. Its discovery (one plant only!) added a new genus and species to New Zealand's flora. It was subsequently propagated by cuttings and seeds and distributed far and wide. A plant regularly flowers in the green-houses of the RHS Gardens, Wisley, Surrey. It grows to at least 10 m in height, with glossy, pinnate (sometimes trifoliate) leaves formed of five broadly oval, blunt-tipped leaflets to 10 cm long. From late spring to late summer, clusters of rather fleshy-textured flowers to 7.5 cm in length open in clusters. In colour they are light yellow but with a hint of green that lends a luminous quality.

Tecomaria (Cape honeysuckle) *Bignoniaceae*

The two or three species that form this genus are native to the southern part of Africa. One is widely grown, *T. capensis* (Zone 9) from S and SE Africa. In the past it has been classified in both *Bignonia* and *Tecoma* and is still sometimes listed under these generic names. Rather a bushy species, it is often seen as a clipped, free-standing bush or hedge, but given moist, rich soil and a humid atmosphere it soon climbs to several metres. It makes a showy pot

147

plant for a cool greenhouse. The dark green, lustrous leaves are pinnate, composed of five to nine broadly ovate, toothed leaflets, which make a fine background for the orange-scarlet flowers. The latter, which appear from spring to autumn, depending on temperature, are carried in short terminal spikes. Each bloom is narrowly trumpet-shaped, about 5 cm long and curved with an asymmetrical gaping mouth and four petal lobes, the upper one deeply cleft.

Testudinaria, see *Dioscorea*.

Tetrapathaea *Passifloraceae*

The one New Zealand species in this genus is essentially an errant passion flower with dioecious flowers, the males having four stamens instead of the passiflora's three. *T. tetrandra* (Zone 9) is a wiry evergreen species growing to 10 m or so, with lustrous, leathery, deep green, ovate to lanceolate leaves up to 7 cm long. The small flowers are yellow-green, solitary or in little clusters and though worthy of close appraisal are rather insignificant. If male and female plants are grown, broadly pear-shaped, 3 cm long bright orange fruits develop. To come upon this liane-like climber looping through the New Zealand bush and hung with a profusion of its bright fruit like Christmas tree decorations, provides an eye-catching sight. But for its dioecious nature this climber must surely have become more popular in cultivation. It will grow in a frost-free greenhouse or even outside in the warmest sites in Britain. It needs humus-rich, preferably acid to neutral soil that is well drained but not dry. Propagation is by seeds in spring or cuttings in summer.

Thladiantha *Cucurbitaceae*

Only one of the 15 species in this genus of tendril climbers from Asia is at all well known. *T. dubia* (Zone 8) is native to China, with a habit of growth similar to that of white bryony (*Bryonia dioica*). It is a herbaceous perennial, rising annually from a sizeable tuberous root to 5 m or more. The harshly-textured, downy leaves are heart-shaped and toothed to 10 cm long. The bright yellow flowers are bell-shaped, about 2.5-3 cm wide, the females often solitary, the males usually clustered, in summer. Female plants produce 2.5-5 cm long ellipsoid fruits with a raised network of longitudinal and latitudinal ribs. This climber can be very showy and looks splendid roaming through a large — but not choice — shrub or over a hedge. Ordinary soil and sun are the cultural requirements. Propagation is by seeds or basal cuttings in spring.

Figure 5.21
Thunbergia alata

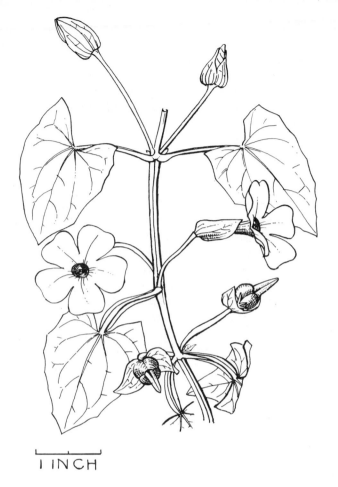

⊢——┴——⊣
I INCH

Thunbergia *Thunbergiaceae* (*Acanthaceae*)

Depending upon the botanical authority, there are between 100 and 200 species of annuals and perennials, many of them climbers, in this African and S Asian genus. They have opposite pairs of simple leaves and showy tubular flowers with five prominent petal lobes. The beaked seed pods are explosive. They thrive in ordinary soil and a sunny site. Propagation is by seeds or layering in spring or cuttings in summer.

T. alata (Zone 5 as annual) (black-eyed Susan) comes from tropical Africa but is naturalised in other warm countries. It is an annual growing to about 3 m in height with triangular-ovate leaves to 7.5 cm long on distinctively winged stalks. From summer to early autumn a succession of 4 cm long flowers arises from the upper leaf axils. Orange-yellow is the usual colour but white and cream forms are available, all with a striking chocolate-purple eye. This is a wonderfully showy half-hardy annual for a sheltered sunny spot.

T. coccinea, see under *T. mysorensis*.

T. gibsonii, see under *T. gregorii*.

T. grandiflora (Zone 9-10, Zone 6 as annual) (*Hexacentris grandiflora*) has a wide natural distribution, from northern India to Burma, Thailand, Cambodia and southern China. It is also widely cultivated in warm countries and in the greenhouses of cooler climates. It is a vigorous woody-stemmed species growing to 10 m or so with angularly margined ovate leaves of rough texture, 10-20 cm long. The blue flowers are about 7.5 cm wide with a yellow throat bearing blue-purple veins. They may be carried singly in the leaf axils or in pendent racemes, mainly during the summer. A white flowered form is known and also darker coloured ones.

T. gregorii (Zone 9, Zone 5 as annual) (tropical Africa) is the correct name for what is usually cultivated as *T. gibsonii*. Both are perennials to about 3 m but are grown as half-hardy annuals in Britain and other temperate countries. *T. gregorii* is similar to *T. alata*, but the flowers are pure orange, 5 cm wide and lack the dark eye. The wings on the leaf stalks and the leaf blades are strongly waved. True *T. gibsonii* has leaf stalks without wings.

T. mysorensis (Zone 9-10) and *T. coccinea* (India) are both woody-stemmed perennials of similar growth habit to *grandiflora* but with much longer floral chains of flowers, those of *mysorensis* 30-45 cm in length. Both have flowers with red, inflated bracts at the base and tubular corollas of yellow and red. In *mysorensis*, however, the enlarged gaping mouth of the 5 cm long flower is pale bright yellow; in *coccinea* the smaller flower is yellow flushed and veined purple and red with bright red lobes. Both need a minimum of 13°C to flourish but provide a spectacular show when growing and flowering well.

Trachelospermum (star jasmine) *Apocynaceae*

Some authorities claim as few as ten, others as many as thirty species for this mainly E Asian genus. Those described are more or less efficient climbers hanging on by both aerial roots and twining stems. They have opposite pairs of oval leaves and small clusters of jasmine-like flowers. A sheltered, moderately sunny wall is necessary if the flowers are to be a feature. Ordinary fertile soil is suitable. Propagation is by cuttings in summer or early autumn, or layering in spring.

T. asiaticum (Zone 9) (*T. divaricatum, crocostemon*) (Japan, Korea) can densely clothe a wall in a very satisfying way with its dark, glossy 2.5-5 cm long leaves. The fragrant 2 cm wide five-lobed flowers open white, ageing yellow. They open in late summer, but are not always borne as freely as one could wish.

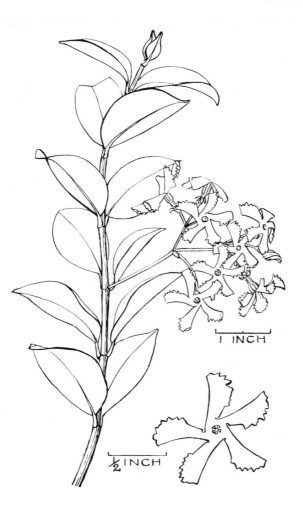

Figure 5.22
Trachelospermum
jasminoides

T. *jasminoides* (Zone 9) (China, Japan) has been known in Britain since 1844 when introduced from Shanghai by Robert Fortune. It is less hardy than *asiaticum* and is more of a twiner than a root clinger, hence needing the support of wires or mesh. When well established, however, it is a taller, superior plant in leaf and flower. The latter are 2.5 cm wide and have long, slender, reflexed calyx lobes (those of *asiaticum* are shorter and erect to more or less spreading). T. *j.* 'Variegatum' has somewhat irregularly margined leaves with creamy-white edges. T. *j. wilsonii* is a Chinese plant with attractively pale-veined, rather narrow leaves that tend to redden in winter.

T. *majus* (Zone 9) (T. *japonicum*) (Japan) has now been plunged into T. *asiaticum* and perhaps in the wild this makes sense. In gardens, however, the plant under this name is highly distinct, with leaves up to 7.5 cm in length, some of which usually turn red in

151

winter. The flowers are somewhat larger and the plant itself more robust, to 18 m in the wild.

Trichosanthes *Cucurbitaceae*

Indo-Malaysia and Australia is the home territory of the 15 species in this genus, only one of which is in general cultivation. *T. cucumerina* (Zone 9-10) (*T. anguina*) is the snake gourd, a species that ranges from India to Australia. It is a tendril climber after the fashion of the bottle gourd (*Lagenaria*) but usually with deeply five to seven-lobed leaves up to 25 cm long. The 5 cm flowers are white, the males in stalked axillary clusters, the females solitary. Each flower is an intriguing object as each of the five petal lobes has a long fringe of curly hairs just like a Victorian parasol. The snaky fruits vary from 30-150 cm in length, very slim in proportion and tapered to a point. They are greenish-white in colour. When young they are boiled and eaten as a vegetable; when mature they are fibrous and bitter. Culture as for *Cucurbita*.

Tripterygium *Celastraceae*

Depending on the botanical authority there are two to five species in this E Asian genus. The two described here are vigorous, deciduous scramblers well worthy of cultivation where there is room. They grow in ordinary soil, ideally humus-enriched, and though they flower and fruit more prolifically in sun, will tolerate a lot of shade. Propagation is by seeds in spring and cuttings in late summer.

T. regelii (Zone 4) (Japan, China, Korea) can reach at least 6 m in height and though it needs some initial tying to its support, makes a luxuriant covering for the wall of a large house. When established, the lateral stems arch down, clad with handsome ovate leaves to 15 cm long. The younger stems are somewhat warted and red-tinted. The leaf stalks are more heavily suffused red. In late summer, large, brown-downy panicles of small, greenish-white five-petalled flowers appear, often in some abundance. They are followed by small greenish fruits with three conspicuous wings.

T. wilfordii (Zone 6) (*T. forrestii*) (Burma, China, Japan, Taiwan) was introduced into Britain in 1913 from China by George Forrest. In overall appearance it is like *T. regelii*, but has the leaf undersides somewhat glaucous, and purple-red fruits. The latter can provide a striking display on a sheltered wall and this species in particular deserves to be grown more often.

Tropaeolum ('nasturtium') *Tropaeolaceae*

This genus has provided the botanist with many problems of classification and the estimated number of species at present hovers between 50 and 90. It is a genus of annual and perennial trailers and climbers, the latter scaling their supports by coiling leaf stalks. The leaves may be simple or compound, the former being generally rounded and peltate — the stalk appearing to be attached to the leaf undersurface. The flowers have five narrow, often coloured, sepals and five petals which may be minute, or large and showy, and a prominent spur, also often coloured. A three-lobed fruit develops which when ripe, splits into three trianguloid sections — the 'seeds' of commerce. Most species require ordinary well-drained soil and a sunny site though some shade is tolerated. *T. speciosum* is an exception, needing at least half shade, acid, preferably peaty soil, and a cool, moist climate. Propagation is by seed when ripe or in spring, or by division of tubers and cuttings in summer.

T. aduncum, see *T. peregrinum*.

T. azureum (Zone 9) (Chile) has also been known as *T. violaeflorum*. It is unique in a genus where the predominant colour of the flowers are shades of red, orange, yellow and white. In Chile it is known as 'violetita de campo' and is a rare plant. For this reason it was all the more exciting to see it in the wild as I did in 1971 when plant collecting with Martyn Cheese and John Watson. Martyn and I were taken to a site in the arid rock-strewn Elqui Valley at about latitude 30° by Professor Muñoz Pizarro. A bad heart did not allow him to toil up the hillside, but he pointed out the area to look. Sure enough there was this almost legendary plant, its frail stems 30-90 cm or so long, trailing over half dead scrub (more or less drought conditions had persisted for some years). The neat little leaves are very slenderly lobed, 1-2.5 cm wide, and from the upper axils, rich purple-blue flowers expand. These are about 2.5 cm wide and rather mimulus-like in shape with a prominent yellow eye. A delightful little climber, but not too easy to grow in Britain and needing greenhouse culture. The small tubers should be re-potted annually in early autumn and kept at a minimum of 7°-10°C for late winter to early spring flowering.

T. brachyceras (Zone 9) (Chile) was introduced by Cheese, Watson and myself under the number BCW 4182. It was identified as such by Professor Muñoz Pizarro, but later on authorities at Kew called it *T. kingii*. Whatever its true status, this tuberous plant resembles a more robust *T. azureum* with beige-yellow flowers; it is intriguing but not especially beautiful.

T. canariense, see *T. peregrinum*.

T. hookeranum (Zone 9) (Chile) is another small tuberous plant that clambers over low scrub, but in this case it comes from the maquis-like coastal scrub of mid-Chile, flowering during the dull 'winter' days of dripping wet sea fog. It is much like the better known *T. tricolorum* in growth, but produces larger, bright yellow flowers with a very mimulus-like appearance and stance, being carried on quite long, erect stalks. It is not difficult to grow in a cool greenhouse, flowering in early spring.

T. lobbianum, see *T. peltophorum*.

T. majus (Zone 5) (Peru) is the very familiar annual nasturtium, the seeds of which are available everywhere. It makes an attractive screen, quickly growing to 2 m or more. It seems likely that at least some of the cultivars available are of hybrid origin with *T. minus*.

T. minus (Zone 5) (Peru) is like a smaller non-climbing version of *majus*, but the flowers have the lower three petals boldly blotched.

T. peltophorum (Zone 5) (*T. lobbianum*) (Colombia, Ecuador) resembles *majus* and is sometimes confused with it, but stems and leaf undersurfaces are downy and the petals are toothed and basally fringed.

T. pentaphyllum (Zone 8) (S America) has large, corky-skinned tubers and slender stems to 3 m or so. As the name suggests, the 2-3 cm wide digitate leaves are composed of five leaflets, the central one much bigger than the others. The 3 cm long flowers have long, thick red spurs at least 2 cm long, purple-striped and spotted palest green sepals and tiny scarlet petals — a fascinating ensemble viewed close to and surprisingly showy *en masse*. The fruits are dark bluish-purple. It blooms from mid to late summer.

T. peregrinum (Zone 5) (*T. aduncum, canariense*) is the well-known Canary creeper. Despite its vernacular name it is a native of Peru where it grows well up in the Andes. It is one of those plants which the Spaniards brought back from S America and acclimatised in the Canary Islands before bringing them into Spain. Presumably it became locally naturalised in its new home and was thought to be native there by visiting British botanists. It is an annual growing to about 4 m with deeply lobed, pale, somewhat greyish-green leaves and bright yellow flowers. Only the up-standing upper two petals of each are fully developed, resembling yellow wings with their broad, feathered tips.

T. polyphyllum (Zone 7-8) (Chile) should not be included here as, in the wild, it is a mat-forming plant of high Andean screes. Curiously enough, however, in cultivation it will push its 1-2 m long stems up through bushes and can be trained as a climber. Foliage-wise alone it would be worth growing, each small, fingered, grey leaf being folded upwards and held rather like the spokes of an umbrella. The end 15-30 cm or more of each stem has crowded, smaller leaves, the axil of every one bearing a quaint pentagonal, pinkish-grey, straight spurred bud attractive in its own right. In early summer each bud expands into a 3 cm wide flower formed of five waved or crimped toothed petals, the upper two rather longer than the lower three. Until the collection made by Cheese, Watson and myself in 1971-2, this species was represented by a pure yellow-flowered clone. It varies in the wild, however, and we were excited to find a few individuals with their upper petals bearing a bold, feathered pattern of orange-crimson veins. Seeds were distributed as BCW 4835A and it is to be hoped that this lovely colour form is still in cultivation.

T. sessilifolium (Zone 8-9) (Chile) is another BCW introduction from the mid-Andean slopes of central Chile. In cultivation it is a scrambler or trailer to about 60 cm with tiny, almost stalkless grey-green fingered leaves. In the wild this tuberous species is variable and in arid areas it is often erect and no more than 10-15 cm tall. The available water supply is undoubtedly a key factor in the way it develops. In shape the flowers are rather like those of *T. majus* but smaller, with white petals, the upper two with a pattern of red veins. It blooms in late spring under glass, later in sheltered sites outside.

T. speciosum (Zone 8) (Chile) has the distinction of being not only the hardiest but the most spectacularly showy of all the cultivated species. Anyone in doubt of this should visit Levens Hall, Kendal, Cumbria, in late summer where this slender climber is a supreme feature, scaling the bizarrely clipped yew trees in the Topiary Garden. It has deep-seated fleshy rhizomes from which the fast-growing stems arise in late spring. The leaves are five to six foliate and neatly disposed. From all the upper leaf axils 4 cm wide vivid vermilion-scarlet flowers expand, setting aflame whatever host plant it favours. Not only are the flowers brightly showy but they are beautifully formed and repay close scrutiny. The two upper petals are wedge-shaped, the three lower are rounded and larger. All have very long stalks, allowing the star-shaped pattern of the sepals to show through and form an eye. Deep blue fruits provide a splendid bonus.

T. tricolorum (Zone 8-9) (*T. tricolor*) grows in the same terrain as *hookeranum* and they are often cheek by jowl, their tubers deep in the rocky soil. Curiously enough the two seem never to have hybridised. In foliage they are similar, but in flower very different. Basically, each flower has a bell or lantern-shaped calyx with a large, broad based, up-curving spur. The spur is invariably red, but the calyx can be red or yellow with a deep maroon mouth. In the wild there are many variations on a theme and the spur can be almost straight to strongly curved. Although a mainly coastal species there is a mountain population which grows just within the winter snow line. This we collected as BCW 4197 and hopefully it is established in Britain where it should be hardy outside.

T. tuberosum (Zone 8, Zone 5 replanted annually) (Bolivia, Peru) is a tuberous rooted half-hardy perennial 2-3 m tall, with rounded greyish-green leaves cleft into three to five broad lobes. The 3-4 cm long flowers, which are poised elegantly on long red stalks, usually have orange-red spurs and sepals and deep to orange-yellow petals, brown-veined within. In its native country this tropaeolum is known as 'anu' and is an item of food. The potato-like tubers are pear-shaped, pale yellow with crimson splashed swollen eyebrows. This large-tubered form was the only one seen in Britain until comparatively recently. It flowered very late in autumn and really needed a greenhouse. However, sometime prior to 1939 a summer flowering form arose and this eventually found its way into the private collection of Mr W.K. Aslet, the former rock garden Superintendent of the RHS Gardens, Wisley. Ken Aslet gave me my first tubers about 30 years ago and I wrote about the plant in the RHS *Journal* (June 1963). As a result of this I distributed many pounds of tubers to the RHS Fellows and to the nurseryman Mr T. Hoog (Van Tubergen) and Alan Bloom (Bressingham Gardens). To distinguish it from the late-flowering clone I proposed the cultivar name 'Ken Aslet' (RHS *The Garden* (August 1981)). This large tubered form has been designated as *T. t. lineomaculata* by the South American botanist Dr Martin Cardenas. The truly wild version of this tropaeolum Dr Cardenas has called *T. t. pilifera*. A few years ago Dr B.K. Blount of Blandford Forum, Dorset, brought back a fine orange form of *T. t. pilifera* and distributed it. It has very long, thin tubers more like rhizomes than true tubers, but otherwise it is just like *T. t. lineomaculata*. To distinguish his orange-flowered clone in cultivation, Dr Blount has bestowed the cultivar name 'Sidney' for Mr Sidney Saunders, an authority on the Peruvian flora.

V

Vitis (grape vine) *Vitidaceae*

Between 50 and 70 species of mainly deciduous tendril climbers are credited to this northern hemisphere genus, the best-known member of which is the grape vine (*V. vinifera*). The species mentioned here have mainly large, rounded, often lobed and maple-like leaves, tiny greenish or yellowish flowers in panicles and berry fruits. They are mainly grown for their ornamental foliage which often takes on bright shades of red, orange and yellow, in autumn. They grow in ordinary fertile soil in sun or shade. Propagation is by cuttings in late summer or autumn *in situ*. Single bud (eye) stem cuttings can also be taken in late winter under glass.

V. aconitifolia, see *Ampelopsis aconitifolia*.

V. amurensis (Zone 4) (eastern USSR, China, Korea) is somewhat similar to *V. vinifera* but distinct in character. It has stems to 10 m and 10-25 cm wide, broadly ovate leaves with three to five more or less deep lobes, the undersides lightly downy. In autumn they take on red and purple shades and a well grown plant can be a striking sight. The small fruits are black.

V. betulifolia (Zone 5) (China) does indeed have birch-shaped

156

leaves though they are larger than any known species of birch. The plant is vigorous, to at least 10 m in height, but has a certain elegance and makes an effective wall covering. In autumn the foliage colours richly and the blue-black fruits are quite showy.

V. X 'Brant' (Zone 4) is sometimes considered to be a cultivar of *V. vinifera*, but its history is, in fact, well documented. It was raised by Mr Charles Arnold of Paris, Ontario, Canada, by crossing *V.* X 'Clinton' (*V. labrusca* X *riparia*) with *V. vinifera* 'Black St Peters'. It favours the *vinifera* parent, but has more shallowly lobed, sharply toothed leaves which in autumn turn bronzy-red and purple with green veins. The dark purple grapes are small, but sweet and aromatic.

V. coignetiae (Zone 5) (Japan, Korea, Sakhalin) is perhaps the most spectacular of all the ornamental vines, soaring into the tops of trees 20 m or more in height, then cascading down. The 15-30 cm long leaves are rounded, often slightly lobed, dark green and almost glossy above, rusty felted beneath. They turn scarlet in autumn and are then immensely showy. The berries are purple-black.

V. davidii (Zone 6) (China) grows to at least 10 m. It is highly distinctive by reason of its stems which are covered with thick, hooked bristles. The leaves are heart-shaped, pointed and toothed, usually with two tiny, pointed side lobes. They vary from 10-25 cm in length and turn crimson in autumn. The small black fruits are pleasantly edible. *V. d. cyanocarpa* has less bristly stems, larger leaves which colour more richly and blue-black fruits.

V. flexuosa major, see *V. pulchra*.

V. inconstans, see *Parthenocissus tricuspidata*.

V. labrusca (Zone 5) (eastern USA) is, in its homeland, known as the fox grape owing to the slightly 'foxy' flavour of its fruit. Leafy and vigorous it grows to 8 m or so, with thick textured leaves which may be toothed or smooth edged, lobed or unlobed, 7-17 cm in length and rusty-downy beneath. The 1.5 cm long grapes are black with a light, waxy patina and of pleasant flavour. This vitis is cultivated for its fruit in eastern USA and adjacent Canada, and there are several superior cultivars, e.g. 'Concord'. It has also been crossed with *V. vinifera* and other species, to produce pest-resistant and hardier fruiting cultivars.

V. piasezkii (Zone 6) (China) resembles and is related to *V. betulifolia*, but the leaves are often somewhat larger and variously three to five-lobed or dissected. A whole range of leaves, from simple to lobed or leafleted can be found on one long stem. In autumn the leaves take on red or bronze shades.

V. pulchra (Zone 5) blends the characters of *V. amurensis* and *coignetiae* and is now generally considered to be a hybrid of this parentage. It has no known wild provenance and was originally sent

157

out as *V. flexuosa major* by the nursery firm of Veitch but is quite distinct from that very rarely cultivated species. *V. pulchra* is a good foliage plant with rounded leaves that are red-tinted when young and turn purple and red prior to falling in autumn.

V. quinquefolia, see *Parthenocissus quinquefolia*.

V. riparia (Zone 2) (eastern and central USA) has the vernacular name of riverbank grape owing to its preference for moist sites by rivers and lakes. In the past it has been known as *V. vulpina*, but this is a confused name now known to embrace *V. riparia*, *cordifolia* and *rotundifolia*. It is a strong grower to 10 m or more, with 7.5-20 cm wide, broadly heart-shaped, bright green leaves, rather variably three-lobed. The flowers have a fragrance reminiscent of mignonette and the grapes are a bright blue-black with a pleasant flavour. Several superior fruiting cultivars, some of them of hybrid origin, are cultivated in the USA and occasionally in Britain.

V. striata, see *Cissus striata*.

V. vinifera (Zone 6) (south eastern and southern central Europe to south western Asia) has been cultivated for thousands of years. It was grown by the ancient Egyptians, Greeks and Romans for fresh fruit and wine making and was introduced to Britain by the Romans. Viticulture continued here, mainly at the monasteries, until their dissolution and in recent years it has seen a revival. In the interim years grape-growing under glass reached a peak of perfection in late Victorian and Edwardian times. *V. vinifera* is a deciduous species growing to 10 m or so with deeply lobed and toothed, rounded leaves to 15 cm wide, the undersides more or less hairy. The fruits can be green to amber-yellow or black-purple, and are juicy and of variable flavour. There are hundreds of fruiting cultivars. *V. v.* 'Apiifolia' ('Laciniosa') has deeply dissected foliage and is known as the parsley vine. 'Purpurea' (Teinurier grape) has the young leaves claret red, the mature ones red-purple. 'Incana' has leaves with whitish-grey down as if thickly covered with remnant spider's webbing. It contrasts very tellingly with its mutant compatriots 'Purpurea' and 'Apiifolia' and looks splendid hung with a purple or red-flowered clematis, e.g. 'Etoile Violette' or 'Ernest Markham'.

W

Wattakaka *Asclepiadaceae*

This genus can also be found under its *Dregea* synonym. Which name is correct seems undecided, though from a purely botanical point of view *Dregea* is conserved over the newer *Wattakaka*. This curious and unlikely name is derived from the native, vernacular wattakaka-kodi, given to the first described species found on the Malabar coast of India. It is closely allied to *Asclepias* and, apart from the twining stems, differs only in small botanical details. *W. sinensis* (Zone 8-9) (China) is the only species likely to be encountered in cultivation. A twining evergreen to about 3 m in height, it has pairs of heart-shaped leaves to 10 cm long, each one sharply pointed and densely velvety-downy beneath. The fragrant summer-borne flowers are carried in nodding, umbel-like clusters on 3-6 cm long stalks. Each flower is about 1.5 cm wide, the five white, red-speckled petals surrounding a central domed stigmatic organ. In overall effect there is a strong resemblance to *Hoya*. As in other members of the *Asclepiadaceae*, the slender seed pods are paired. This quietly attractive plant was introduced by E.H. Wilson in 1907. It had, however, first been discovered by Augustine Henry close to the Ichang Gorge of the Yangtse River in 1887. At about the same time, the Reverend E. Faber found it higher up the river. Later, Camillo Schneider established its occurrence on the upper Yangtse at an altitude of 2400 metres. Ordinary well-drained fertile soil is suitable, but a sheltered site, preferably a south west wall, is essential for continuing success. Propagation is by seed in spring or cuttings in late summer.

Wisteria (*Wistaria*) *Leguminosae*

Along with the honeysuckles, clematis and climbing roses, this genus makes up a quartet of the best known and loved climbing plants, at least in Britain. About nine to ten species names are listed, but only three are widely cultivated. All three are Asiatic, the equivalent one to two species from the eastern USA not thriving so well in cool summer climates. All species are typified by ash-like pinnate leaves and dangling racemes of pea-shaped flowers like those of laburnum. The seed pods are bean-like. Ordinary fertile, well-drained soil is suitable, and a sunny site results in more profuse flowering. Growth is rapid in the early years and flowering can be delayed by as much as ten years while a framework of stems is built up. Once the plant has filled its allotted space, all young climbing stems should be cut back to three to four basal leaves at regular intervals from late summer onwards. This helps to build up flowering spurs. Propagation is by layering in spring or cuttings in late summer with bottom heat 18°-21°C. Seed can also be sown (in spring) but the results are variable and many years may elapse before flowering starts.

W. floribunda (Zone 4) (*W. brachybotrys*) (Japan) can achieve 10 m or so in a dead tree and looks quite splendid in such a situation. It has leaves composed of 13-19 ovate leaflets, each 4-8.5 cm long and a semi-lustrous dark green. The 13-25 cm long racemes bear 2 cm long violet to purple-blue flowers in early summer. The 8-15 cm pods are velvety-downy. The stems twine clockwise, a clear distinction from the similar *W. sinensis* which coils the opposite way. *W. f.* 'Alba' has white flowers sometimes with faint lilac overtones. There appear to be clones with short and long racemes, the latter rather shy flowering. 'Issai' may be a hybrid with *sinensis*, having the jizz of that species, but the clockwise spiralling stems of *floribunda*. (In the USA, however, the clone known as 'Issai' is described as having stems that spiral in both directions). The usual clone under this name in Britain has lilac-blue flowers in racemes to 25 cm long and leaves with mostly 13 leaflets. 'Issai Perfect' has racemes of slightly paler flowers to 38 cm long and leaves with 15 leaflets. 'Macrobotrys' (*W. multijuga*) has blue-purple tinted lilac flowers in racemes to 1 m long. Under ideal conditions this is the most spectacular of all the wisterias; racemes 1.8 m long have been recorded in Japan. 'Rosea' (*W. multijuga rosea*) bears flowers with pale pink standard petals and purple keels. 'Violacea' has violet-blue blossoms. 'Violacea Plena' has the limited distinction of being double-flowered. It has violet-purple rosetted flowers, not very freely produced.

W. X *formosa* (Zone 5) is the name given to hybrids between *W. floribunda* and *sinensis*. The original plant sometimes sold under this name was raised in Professor Sargent's garden in Massachusetts, USA, in 1905. It favours *sinensis*, with 25 cm long racemes of pale violet flowers that open simultaneously, and leaves with 9-15 leaflets. See also comments under *W. floribunda* 'Issai'.

W. frutescens (Zone 5) is the only N American species likely to be encountered in British gardens and even here is rare. It grows to 12 m or more in the wild, with leaves composed of 9-17 ovate leaflets, each 4-6 cm in length. Mauve, yellow-eyed flowers open in crowded, 10-15 cm long racemes in summer. The pods are smooth and much less flattened than the Asiatic species. Although later flowering than *floribunda* and *sinensis*, it is a much less effective plant. *W. f. macrostachys* (*W. macrostachys*) has longer, finer racemes and is a worthy garden plant deserving to be grown more often.

W. sinensis (Zone 5) (*W. chinensis*) can reach the tops of trees 18 m or more in height. It has stems that twine with an anti-clockwise motion and leaves composed of 9-13 elliptic to oblong, 3.5-7.5 cm long leaflets. The individual flowers are about 2.5 cm long, mauve to deep lilac, and fragrant, in racemes to 30 cm in length. They open in spring with the unfurling leaves and, unlike *floribunda*, all the flowers in a raceme open more or less simultaneously. The seed pods are velvety, 13-15 cm long, rather wider at the tip than the base. This is the most widely grown of all the wisterias. It was introduced from the garden of a Chinese merchant in Canton at the instigation of John Reeves, Chief Inspector of tea in that city. The first two plants reached Britain in 1816, and it seems likely that most of the plants in gardens today are descended from them. *W. s.* 'Alba' has white flowers. 'Black Dragon' bears dark purple, double flowers. 'Plena' has lilac double flowers of rosetted form. 'Prolific' ('Oosthoek's Variety') is an especially free-blooming selection.

W. venusta (*W. brachybotrys*) (Zone 5) (Japan) can climb to 10 m and has leaves formed of 9-13 downy leaflets, each one up to 9 cm in length. The broad racemes of slightly fragrant white flowers are 10-15 cm long and open in early summer. This is an example of a species founded upon a cultivated albino cultivar. *W. v. violacea* is the true wild species with violet-purple flowers. In the standard *Flora of Japan* by Ohwi, *W. venusta violacea* is given the name *W. brachybotrys* and *W. venusta* itself *W. b.* 'Alba', a far more sensible approach to this nomenclatural problem. This is the best of the white-flowered wisterias and looks particularly effective against a dark, red brick wall or trained up a tall tree stump.

APPENDIX

List of Climbers for Special Purposes

Where plants are given a hardiness zone classification less than that of Britain (7-8), American works of reference have been consulted.

Cold
Resistant
Plants

Zone 2
Celastrus scandens
Clematis verticillaris
Parthenocissus inserta
Vitis riparia

Zone 3
Apios americana
Lathyrus odoratus
Parthenocissus quinquefolia

Zone 4
Actinidia arguta
A. kolomitka
A. polygama
Ampelopsis brevipedunculata
Aristolochia macrophylla
Campsis radicans
C. × tagliabuana
Celastrus articulatus
Clematis aethusifolia
C. fusca
C. × jouiniana
C. texensis
C. virginiana
C. vitalba
C. viticella
Hydrangea anomala petiolaris
Lonicera periclymenum
L. sempervirens
Menispermum canadense
Parthenocissus tricuspidata

Polygonum aubertii
P. baldschuanicum
Rosa canina
Rubus laciniatus
R. ulmifolius
Smilax rotundifolia
Vitis amurensis
V. × 'Brandt'
Wisteria floribunda

Zone 5
Actinidia melanandra
Akebia trifoliata
Ampelopsis bodinieri
Aristolochia tomentosa
Cardiospermum halicacabum (as annual)
Clematis – most deciduous species and cultivars
Coccolus carolinus
C. trilobus
Convolvulus sepium
Dolichos lablab (as annual)
Euonymus fortunei radicans
Hedera colchica
H. helix
Ipomoea bona-nox (as annual)
I. coccinea
I. nil
I. purpurea
I. quamoclit
I. tricolor

162

Jasminum nudiflorum
Lathyrus latifolius
Lonicera alseuosmoides
L. × americana
L. caprifolium
L. flava
L. × heckrottii
L. henryi
Phaseolus caracalla (an annual)
Rosa setigera — and hybrids derived from it
Rubus phoenicaulasius
Schizandra chinensis
Schizophragma hydrangeoides
Thunbergia alata (as annual)

Zone 5
Euonymus fortunei radicans
Hedera colchica
H. helix
Lonicera alseuosmoides

Zone 6
Hedera rhombea
Lonicera japonica
Rubus henryi

Zone 7
Clematis armandii
C. cirrhosa
Decumaria sinensis
Fatshedera lizei
Gelsemium
Hedera napaulensis
Holboellia coriacea
Pileostegia
Rubus flagelliflorus
Stauntonia hexaphylla

Zone 8
Araujia
Aristolochia sempervirens
Asteranthera
Berberidopsis
Doxantha
Ercilla

T. gregorii (as annual)
Tropaeolum majus
T. minus
T. peregrinum
T. tuberosum (tubers lifted annually)
Vitis betulifolia
V. coignetiae
V. labrusca
V. pulchra
Wisteria × formosa
W. frutescens
W. sinensis
W. venusta

Eustrephus
Hedera canariensis
Hydrangea serratifolia
Jasminum mesnyi
J. floridum
Kadsura
Mutisia decurrens
M. oligodon
Schizandra propinqua
Watakaka

Zone 9
Anredera
Antigonon
Asparagus
Beaumontia
Bignonia
Bomarea
Cissus
Clytostoma
Cobaea
Distictis
Dolichos
Ficus pumila
Hibbertia
Hoya carnosa
Opomoea acuminata
Jasminum angulare
J. azoricum
J. lineare

Evergreen
Climbers
by Zone

163

J. nitidum
J. polyanthum
Kennedia
Lapageria
Lardizabala
Lonicera hildebrandiana
Manettia
Mikania
Mutisia slematis
M. ilicifolia
Pandorea

Plumbago auriculata
Pyrosegia venusta
Rhodochiton
Solandra
Tecomaria
Tetrapathaea
Trachelospermum

Zone 10
  Allamanda
  Stephanotis

Annual or Biennial Climbers (or grown as such)

Adlumia
Araujia
Asarina
Cardiospermum
Cobaea
Cucurbita
Dolichos
Eccremocarpus
Humulus

Ipomoea
Lathyrus
Mina
Momordica
Oxypetalum
Phaseolus
Thunbergia
Tropaeolum

Small-Growing Climbers (under 3 m · or easily kept so)

Aconitum
Adlumia
Anredera
Asarina
Asteranthera
Berberidopsis
Bomarea
Cardiospermum
Clematis (some)
Clianthus
Cocculus
Codonopsis
Cucurbita
Dolichos
Eccremocarpus
Ercilla
Euonymus
× *Fatshedera*
Ficus
Hedera (some)

Humulus
Ipomoea
Jasminum (some)
Kadsura
Lapageria
Lathyrus
Lonicera (some)
Mina
Muehlenbeckia
Mutisia
Oxypetalum
Rosa (some)
Rubus
Solanum
Sollya
Thladiantha
Thunbergia (some)
Trachelospermum
Tropaeolum

For Trees

Actinidia
Akebia

Ampelopsis
Celastrus

Clematis (some)
Ercilla
Hedera
Hydrangea
Parthenocissus
Polygonum

Rosa (some)
Schizophragma
Tripterygium
Vitis
Wisteria

Asteranthera
Berberidopsis
Campsis
Clematis
Clianthus
Cobaea
Decumaria
Eccremocarpus
Ercilla
Euonymus
Ficus
Halboellia
Hedera
Hydrangea

Jasminum
Kadsura
Lapageria
Lonicera
Parthenocissus
Passiflora
Pileostegia
Rosa
Schizandra
Solanum
Stauntonia
Trachelospermum
Vitis
Wisteria

For Walls

Ampelopsis
Anredera
Aristolochia macrophylla
A. sempervirens
Asteranthera
Clematis
Cucurbita
Decumaria
Ercilla
Euonymus
X *Fatschedera*
Ficus
Hedera
Hydrangea

Lagenaria
Lathyrus latifolius
Lonicera
Paederia
Parthenocissus
Phaseolus
Pileostegia
Rosa
Schizophragma
Thladiantha
Trachelospermum
Tropaeolum
Vitis

For Ground
Cover

Allamanda
Anredera
Antigonon
Aristolochia (some)
Asarina
Asparagus
Beaumontia
Bignonia
Bomarea

Bougainvillea
Bowiea
Canarina
Ceropegia
Cissus (some)
Clianthus
Dioscorea
Distictis
Doxantha

For Greenhouse
Culture in
Zones 1 to 8

Eustrephus
Ficus
Gelsemium
Gloriosa
Hardenbergia
Hibbertii
Hoya
Jasminum (some)
Kennedia
Lagenaria
Lapageria
Littonia
Lonicera (some)
Mandevilla
Manettia
Maurandya
Mikania
Momordica
Pandorea
Passiflora

Petrea
Plumbago
Podranea
Pyrostegia
Rhodochiton
Sandersonia
Senecio
Smilax
Solandra
Solanum
Sollya
Stephanotis
Streptosolen
Tecomanthe
Tecomaria
Tetrapathaea
Thunbergia
Trichosanthes
Tropaeolum (some)

Flower Colour

Blue-purple

Aconitum
Asarina antirrhiniflora
A. scandens
Clematis (some)
Clitostoma
Cobaea
Codonopsis
Dolichos
Ipomoea
Lathyrus magellanicus
L. odoratus (some)
L. pubescens

Oxypetalum caeruleum
Passiflora X allardii
P. caerulea
P. X *caeruleoracemosa*
P. X *caponii*
P. quadrangularis
P. umbilicata
Petrea volubilis
Plumbago auriculata
Thunbergia grandiflora
Tropaeoleum azureum
Wisteria

Red-pink

Antigonon
Asarina barclaiana
A. erubescens
Asteranthera
Berberidopsis
Bomarea edulis
Bougainvillea (some)
Clematis (some)
Clianthus puniceus
Convolvulus althaeoides

C. elegantissimus
Dichelostemma volubilis
Distictis
Eccremocarpus scaber
    carmineus
Gloriosa
Hardenbergia
Ipomoea coccinea
I. hederacea
I. nil

166

I. quamoclit
Jasminum beesianum
J. × stephanense
Kennedia coccinea
K. rubicunda
Lapageria
Lathyrus latifolius
L. odoratus (some)
L. rotundifolius
Lonicera × americana
L. × brownii
L. sempervirens
Mandevilla sanderi
M. splendens
Manettia inflata

Mina lobata
Mutisia ilicifolia
M. oligodon
Pandorea jasminoides
Passiflora antioquensis
P. coccinea
P. × exoniensis
P. mollissima
Podranea ricasoliana
Rhodochiton atrosanguineum
Rosa (some)
Thunbergia coccinea
T. mysorensis
Tropaeolum speciosum
T. tuberosum

Araujia
Beaumontia
Bougainvillea (some)
Clematis (some)
Clianthus puniceus 'Albus'
Codonopsis convolvulacea
　　'Alba'
Decumaria
Hoya carnosa
Hydrangea
Ipomoea bona-nox
Jasminum angulare
J. dispermum

J. lineare
J. nitidum
J. officinale
J. polyanthum
Lagenaria
Mandevilla boliviensis
M. laxa
Pandorea jasminoides
P. pandorana
Rosa (some)
Schizophragma
Stephanotis
Trachelospermum

White

Allamanda
Bignonia
Bomarea caldasii
Bougainvillea (some)
Campsis
Canarina
Clematis (some)
Cucurbita
Doxantha
Eccremocarpus
Gelsemium
Hibbertia
Jasminum floridum
J. mesnyi
J. nudiflorum

J. subhumile
Kadsura
Littonia
Lonicera etrusca
L. flava
L. × heckrottii
L. hildebrandiana
L. periclymenum
L. sempervirens 'Sulphurea'
L. × tellmanniana
L. tragophylla
Mutisia clematis
M. decurrens
Pyrostegia venusta
Rosa (some)

Yellow-orange

Sandersonia aurantiaca
Senecio confusus
Solandra
Streptosolen
Teconaria
Thladiantha

Thunbergia alata
T. gregorii
Tropaedolum majus
T. peregrinum
T. polyphyllum
T. tuberosum 'Ken Aslet'

Fragrance and Fruit

Fragrance

Actinidia arguta
Anredera
Apios
Beaumontia
Clematis afoliata
C. armandii
C. hookerana
Clematoclethra integrifolia
Holboellia
Hoya carnosa
Ipomoea bona-nox
Jasminum angulare
J. lineare
J. nitidum
J. officinale

J. polyanthum
Lathyrus odoratus
Lonicera X *americana*
L. caprifolium
L. etrusca
L. hildebrandiana
L. japonica
L. periclymenum
Pandorea pandorana
Podranea ricasoliana
Rosa (various)
Stephanotis
Trachelospermum
Wisteria

Fruit

Actinidia chinensis
Akebia quinata
A. trifoliata
Billardiera
Cardiospermum
Celastrus
Clematis aethusifolia
C, alpina
C. cirrhosa
C. X *durandii*
C. grata
C. orientalis
C. songarica
C. tangutica
C. vitalba
Cocculus
Cucurbita
Dolichos
Jasminum beesianum
Kadsura japonica

Lagenaria
Lardizabala
Menispermum
Momordica
Passiflora
Periploca
Rosa – some species and culti-
vars
Rubus – some species and
cultivars
Sinofranchetia
Sinomenium
Tecomanthe dendrophila
Tetrapathaea
Trichosanthes
Tripterygium wilfordii
Vitis X 'Brandt'
V. Labrusca
V. riparia
V. vinifera

The Author's Top Fifty

Atinidia kolomikta
Akebia quinata
*Allamanda catharctica**
*Asteranthera ovata**
Berberidopsis corallina
*Bomarea coldasii**
Bougainvillea X *buttiana* 'Mrs
  Butt'*
Bougainvillea glabra 'Variegata'*
Campsis X *tagliabuana* 'Mme
  Galen'
Celastrus orbiculatus
Clematis armandii 'Snowdrift'
Clematis 'Hagley Hybrid'
Clematis montana grandiflora
Clematis tangutica
Clematis viticella 'Rubra'
Clematis 'W.E. Gladstone'
*Clianthus puniceus**
Eccremocarpus scaber
Euonymus fortunei radicans
  'Variegatus'
*Gloriosa rothschildiana**
*Hardenbergia comptonia**
Hedera colchica 'Dentata varie-
  gata'
Hedera 'Ravensholst'
*Hoya carnosa**
Hydrangea anomala petiolaris
*Jasminum polyanthum**

*Lapageria rosea**
*Mutisia decurrens**
Pileostegia viburnoides
*Plumbago auriculata**
*Rhodochiton atrosanguinea**
Rosa 'Albertine'
Rosa filipes 'Kiftsgate'
Rosa 'Madame Gregoire
  Staechelin'
Rosa 'Mermaid'
Rosa 'New Dawn'
Rosa soulieana
*Sandersonia aurantiaca**
*Schizandra grandiflora rubri-
  flora*
*Senecio confusus**
Solanum crispum
*Stephanotis floribunda**
*Streptosolen jamesonii**
Tripterygium wilfordii
Tropaeolum speciosum
Tropaeolum tuberosum
Vitis coignetiae
Vitis vinifera 'Incana'
Wisteria floribunda 'Macro-
  botrys'
Wisteria sinensis

*Greenhouse or protected in
zones 1-8.

Index

173

Index

Index